Interests of Future Korean-American Leaders

Edited by
Minjae Kim

The Hermit Kingdom Press
Highland Park * Seoul * Bangalore * Cebu

Interests of Future Korean-American Leaders
Copyright ©2010 The Hermit Kingdom Press

Hardcover ISBN13: 978-1-59689-102-9
Paperback ISBN13: 978-1-59689-260-6

Write To Address:
The Hermit Kingdom Press
P. O. Box 1226
Highland Park, NJ 08904-1226
The United States of America

Library of Congress Cataloging-in-Publication Data

Interests of future Korean-American leaders / edited by Minjae Kim.
    p. cm.
Includes bibliographical references.
ISBN 978-1-59689-102-9 (hardcover : alk. paper) -- ISBN 978-1-59689-260-6 (pbk. : alk. paper)
I. Kim, Minjae.
AC5.I692 2010
973'.04957--dc22

                             2010042688

Dedicated to New York University

Contents

Acknowledgement

I want to acknowledge several people that have been important in my life and hence my intellectual journey:

- Sincere thanks to my mother, father, sister, grandmother, and grandfather for being the best family anyone could ever have.
- Thanks to Professor Christian Kim of Asia Evangelical College and Seminary for unending support.
- Thanks to my best friends including but not limited to (alphabetical) Amber, Cindy, Erik, Hannah, Jaewon, Julie, and Margot for every good reason I can possibly think of.
- Thanks to one of my best friends, Tyler Clementi, for having supported me through the hard times, and also condolence for the family who recently lost the trustworthy and talented individual that will forever be in my heart.
- Sincere thanks to my Father, the One and Only.

Introduction

I dreamed a dream in time gone by…
Then I was young and unafraid
And dreams were made and used and wasted
There was no ransom to be paid
No song unsung, no wine untasted…

The authors of these essays are young writers who were unafraid to extend their intellectual horizons through intensive research and writing over the course of a few months. As the last few months—and especially the last two weeks—have been quite a turbulent period for my life, I empathize with Fantine as she desperately sings her emotions in *Les Misérables* and reminisces her good old times. I think back to how absorbed I became in reading about contemporary issues in China, and how blessed I was to have an opportunity to learn about the issues. I became more of a critical thinker in reading texts and understanding current events.

For me, to live out my dream has always been to learn. I *may* stop attending school at some point of my life, but I will never stop learning—from other people, events, and myself. I am often surprised by what I can come up with and to how much extent I can achieve. But learning has only come when I had faith in myself…

These young writers are incredibly talented individuals who believed in their potentials when they wrote these essays. They spoke of what they were truly passionate about and wanted to share the fruits of their learning with others. These projects are stepping-stones for most of these writers to start writing more prodigious materials that can have great impacts in diverse areas, including medicine, economy, and history.

These are the young leaders of the coming generation that are living out their dreams by learning and daring to speak up. Dreaming is not for an idealist; dreaming is for a leader who has the potential to make a difference. And these young scholars have only just realized their potentials.

Minjae Kim
New York University
New York, NY

"Tiger's Wings: Illusion of China?"

Minjae Kim
New York University

There has never been a nation like China. The heterogeneous yet jingoistic society of 1.33 billion people has no equivalent in the history of mankind. Despite its continued categorization as a developing country, China's exorbitant rate of gross domestic product growth has outperformed those of all developed nations for the past 32 years (Kynge xii). In 2006, more than 400 million people were lifted above their poverty line by one U.S. dollar a day. According to a New York Times article on August 15, 2010, China is expected to surpass the United States as the world's largest economy as early as 2030.[1] Its vast resources of human capital and rare metals[2] equip China as a formidable player in world economy and politics, as if "adding wings to a tiger" like the Chinese adage: "Ru Hu Tian Yi 如虎添翼".

The auspicious implication in the apothegm seems to reflect China's prospective economic growth. A closer examination of China's position in the world and situation within its borders, however, projects a different image of the tiger: it propels forward with broken wings, trying to leap but only stomping all over the ground in the process. The Communist Party's partial reforms in economy and no change in politics leave the state in a tumult, more unstable than ever underneath the veneer of stability. Political, social, and economic protests are staged incessantly, only to be suppressed and penalized by

---

[1] David Barboza, "China Passes Japan as Second-Largest Economy," *New York Times*, 15 Aug 2010, 15 Aug 2010, <http://www.nytimes.com/2010/08/16/business/global/16yuan.html?_r=2&scp=2&sq=China&st=cse>.
[2] China is the third richest country in minerals, having about 153 minerals confirmed in 2000. Haiwang Yuan, *This Is China: the First 5,000 Years* (Great Barrington, MA: Berkshire Pub. Group, 2010), 8.

the People's Liberation Army, who no longer "liberates" the people[3] but only answers to the Communist Party. The number of "mass incidents," the euphemism for strikes, demonstrations, and protests coined by the Ministry of Public Security,[4] has accelerated every year. There were 127,000 in 2008,[5] and 58,000 similarly reported demonstrations in only the first three months of 2009.[6] The propaganda department can no longer contain the economic impediments and political discontent; the frenzied commotion is exposed to the international network through audacious blogs, websites, and newspapers. Underneath the leaping tiger is an inconceivable mess of dissatisfied people and deteriorating environment. Despite its semblance of powerful economy and centralized power, China's volatile economy and politics evince that the Communist Party cannot rule for long unless it adjusts to the demands of the changing society and institutes reforms to rectify the current turmoil within the state.

China's propitious economy can be justified by Deng Xiaoping's program of reform called "Gaige Kaifang 改革開放," which literally means "reform and opening." In order to "transform China into a nation capable of assuming a leading role in world politics," the new leader addressed Four Modernizations in the order of agriculture, industry, science and technology, and military (Godwin 27). One instrumental change precipitated by Deng Xiaoping was the establishment of Special Economic Zones in the 1980s. Special Economic Zones engaged

---

[3] The original stance of the People's Liberation Army was to support the Communist Party in liberating the people from the oppressive and corrupt Nationalist Party.

[4] Weilan Wang, "Making Sense of 'Mass Incidents'". *Global Times, Special Report,* 30 May 2009, 08 Aug. 2010 <http://special.globaltimes.cn/2009-05/433271.html>.

[5] Equivalent of 348 a day. Andrew Wedeln, "Enemies of the State: Mass Incidents and Subversion in China". *APSA 2009 Toronto Meeting Paper,* 13 Aug. 2009, 08 Aug. 2010 <Available at SSRN: http://ssrn.com/abstract=1451828>.

[6] The annual equivalent would present an increase of 105,000 from the previous year: "58,000 Mass Incidents in China in First Quarter as Unrest Grows to Largest Ever Recorded." *Libcom.org.* 6 May 2009. Web. 02 Aug. 2010. <http://libcom.org/news/58000-mass-incidents-china-first-quarter-unrest-grows-largest-ever-recorded-06052009>.

China in international trade effectively by deviating from the command economy of the state. "Those who brought businesses into the zone received generous tax breaks" (Fishman 88), encouraging foreign companies to partner with China and provide direct investment. It was a strategic plan for a nation to acquire the latest technology and finance the development in China. Shenzhen, the first Special Economic Zone established in 1980, experienced rapid growth that has no perfect historical analogue. After only 25 years, Shenzhen's population exceeded seven million. Its economy was ranked the fourth largest in the country, and per capita output among the highest in the country (Fishman 88). With joint ventures milking the economy, [7] Shenzhen's development foreshadowed greater China's industrialization within the boundaries and worldwide.

Another fundamental change that Deng's "Gaige Kaifang" warranted was de-collectivization of agricultural land. Mao Zedong's unduly idealistic socialism had required collectivization of all land and property, including animals and farm tools. The government reasoned that bigger, unified tracts could be farmed more efficiently, and modern farm equipment could be employed insofar as such technology was available (Fishman 43). Collectivization eradicated a myriad of small enterprises and their incentives to produce more--why should one work harder than a neighbor if one will obtain the same pay at the end? In the 1970s, eighteen farmers in Xiaogang of Anhui Province covertly challenged the norm of collectivization. The farmers were among the most destitute on earth, with annual incomes of only $2.50 a year. Struggling for survival, they agreed to sell or barter whatever surplus they could gather after paying a collective grain tax and keep the proceeds. Deng noticed their illicit activities, but ultimately endorsed the idea because it reduced peasant poverty at almost no cost to the government (Fishman 47). The new 'household responsibility

---

[7] As discussed in Fishman's fifth chapter, "Meet George Jetson in Beijing," joint ventures were a primary method of importing advanced foreign technology with foreign direct investment. Foreign companies that recognized the potential of Chinese market took this opportunity to invest and produce without regular trade restrictions such as tariff barriers.

system,' declared to be the national norm in 1983, allowed families to sell all above-quota output to the government at a price above the price for quota output or sell the surplus in local markets, or consume it themselves. In 1985, Deng removed the old system of quota procurement for all agricultural crops and also promised to buy all surplus output at or above the fixed floor prices. These agricultural reforms created incentives to produce more, and eventuated as a monumental success.

> From 1978 to 1984, the output of grain per head of the (total) population grew by an average of 3.8 per cent per year (compared with 0.2 per cent between 1957 and 1977), the output of cotton by 17.5 per cent (compared with a fall of 0.6 per cent) and the output of meat by 9.0 per cent (compared with 1.7 per cent). Rural consumption per head, having grown by only a third between 1965 and 1978, almost trebled between 1978 and 1986 (Evans 254).

Despite the new system's contradiction with Mao's ideal of collectivization and "equality," Deng argued that "Poverty is not socialism" and "To get rich is glorious" (Chang 9), promoting more economic growth.

Institutions of Special Economic Zones and household responsibility system capture a glimpse of China's rudimentary transformations into a more open, more prosperous nation. China's entry into the World Trade Organization in September 2001 illustrates China's initiative to advance its economic position in the world. And as it is more integrated into the global economy, China is taking the center stage. Erskine Bowels, a chief of staff in the White House under Bill Clinton, said in 2004, "China has an unfair advantage. They don't pay anything... not for their equipment or buildings. We can't compete with that."[8] Chinese government subsidizes water and electric energy, and offer cheap loans, often with little

---

[8] Tim Wilkins, "Bowels Finds Support in Robeson Fund-Raiser," *Lumberton (NC) Robesonian*, July 1, 2004.

expectation of reimbursement (Fishman 152). Hence, many in the business world use the term "China price" interchangeably with the "lowest price possible (Fishman 177). With the cheapest price available, customers from all over the world have increased purchasing power parity and standard of living, which makes China the hero of today's world economy.

The romantic outlook, however, may be a fallacy based on cursory examination of data. With cheap labor and products, China is taking over the economy, rather than fostering its growth. China is outsourcing the world: there are fewer jobs, and lower wages for the rest of us. Because millions of Chinese people are willing to work (many more hours) with much less wages, factories are moving to China, and jobs abroad shifting their employees. China is supplying both the materials and human labor at entrancing prices. The search for the evidence is not too difficult; the vogue is "Made in China."

Wal-Mart, the world's largest private employer, appropriately has followed the trend and taken advantage of the China price. Wal-Mart used to boast that nearly all its products were "made in America" in 1995, with only six percent of the merchandise imported from abroad. In 2004, however, more than 80 percent of the worldwide Wal-Mart factories had Chinese suppliers (Fishman 154). As Wal-Mart has endeavored to reduce the prices of their products every year, Wal-Mart's competitors as well as suppliers are going out of business and consequently losing myriad of jobs.

Mid-size American companies such as Signicast and Milwaukee Valve Company Ltd. are relocating their factories out of cities and into rural areas, or into China--and with those factories, *millions* of jobs. Milwaukee, Wisconsin is not the only city that is adversely affected by the migration of workplaces: "Once proud industrial centers, such as Buffalo, Detroit, and Philadelphia" are losing three-quarters of their manufacturing jobs (Fishman 190). Goldman Sachs, the world's premier investment bank, predicted that 6 million jobs would leave the United States by 2013, at a cost of $150 billion in wages to

Americans.[9] Milwaukee Valve Company Ltd. is now located at the "End of Guangrui Road" in Wuxi, a city about an hour and half northwest from Shanghai. It operates with cheap trucks, low mechanical bills, and workers who devote more time for much lower wages; and thus the company is able to sustain its business (Fishman 191). There are, of course, many more enterprises to which China caters these services.

The German Volkswagen (Fishman 165) and Japanese Toyota, Sony, Panasonic, and Toshiba had "realized long ago that Chinese factories could beat them on price and that they needed to move production there to survive" (Fishman 170-1). Because of the migration of factories, the Mexican Ministry of Labor reported that country's workers earned less in 2005 than they did in 1993 (Fishman 149). Multitudinous companies seeking China for cheap yet diligent labor, subsidized energy, and inexpensive resources and facilities thence increase the growth of the nation's labor market, GDP, and export. China's growth may be raising the standard of living worldwide by providing quality products at cheaper prices, but as a result, many nations suffer by losing jobs and customers.

China's gargantuan human capital[10] has been integral in restructuring the world economy--not only by absorbing factories and jobs, but also directly by replacing workers in other nations with its massive migration. Many of them travel illegally, understanding the dangers but desperate to earn money to send back home. In June 2000, the 58 Chinese immigrants found asphyxiated in a cargo at Dover alarmed the world. They had tried to cross over to Britain after a "snakehead" (Chinese

---

[9] University of California Haas School of Business, press release, "UC Berkeley Study Assesses Potential Impacts of 'Second Wave' of Outsourcing Jobs from U.S.," October 29, 2003, http://www.haas.berkeley.de/news/20031029_outsourcing.html

[10] Mao Zedong argued that big population represents strength of a powerful nation, averring that every mouth is attached to two arms; people could always produce more than they consumed. The result? 582.6 million in 1953 to about 1.33 billion now (even after Deng instituted One-Child-Policy three years ago). James Kynge, *China Shakes the World: a Titan's Breakneck Rise and Troubled Future and the Challenge for America* (Boston: Houghton Mifflin, 2006), 50-1.

title for a director of illegal transportation) had organized for months.[11] The incident ensued a crackdown in Fuqing and increased the price of passage, but did not discourage the number of illegal immigrations. The cost differentials between China and European country were too great; for instance, the immigrants in Prato, Italy earned ten times what they used to in Wenzhou, China (Kynge 84).

American journalist James Kynge interviewed one of the immigrants named Huang, who paid another $3,000 (after the Dover incident) on top of the $12,000 he had already handed over for his trip. Huang's father had been imprisoned because of the father's own debt, and thus Huang risked all of his and his extended family's properties as collaterals as he borrowed for his trip. He worked in Sicily, Bologna, Rome, and Prato to settle the debts. In April 2005, he was almost debt-free, but could not go back home because his son's school fees were too expensive. Not having seen his family once since he left, Huang tried to comfort himself, "Everything is for my son" (Kynge 80). Many Chinese in desperate situations like Huang's have been replacing the workers in Europe. Some of these illegal immigrants even become entrepreneurs themselves. Like Wang Yihua of Great Fashion, they set up businesses on their own, utilize cheap Chinese factories and sell the same quality products at much cheaper prices, endangering their old employers' businesses in Italy[12] (Kynge 84). The massive Chinese workforce was now producing the bosses outside China.

Within the state boundaries, there are many bosses and entrepreneurs arising. Edward Tian, the founder of AsiaInfo and the earliest director of China Netcom Company, has been optimistic about how his ambition to wire all of China with high bandwidth can affect those even without personal computers because they can come in contact through the education system.

---

[11] Hyland, Julie. "58 Chinese Migrants Found Dead in Lorry at Dover, Britain." World Socialist Web Site. 21 June 2000. Web. 30 Sept. 2010. <http://www.wsws.org/articles/2000/jun2000/immi-j21.shtml>.

[12] "Of the six thousand or so textile companies that existed in 2000, fewer than half remained in mid-2005." James Kynge, *China Shakes the World: a Titan's Breakneck Rise and Troubled Future and the Challenge for America* (Boston: Houghton Mifflin, 2006), 84.

David Sheff, the author of *China Dawn* details the firsthand accounts of Edward Tian and several venture capital entrepreneurs who have earned millions of dollars through their aspirations and perseverance. David Sheff and many other foreign journalists encounter countless educated, talented, and ambitious individuals in China that create inventions within weeks and overwork themselves to the maximum capacity. Edward Tian's inspirational speeches talk of advancing China and taking part in history to be remembered by all the following generations. There seems to be too much potential, dream, and hope for China.

The optimistic accounts on the surface engender a common misconception in the west that "the growing ranks of private entrepreneurs in China represent a force for democratic change in the country" (Pan 155). Some cases undeniably support this assumption: Edward Tian's AsiaInfo[13] and China Netcom Corporation [14] were met with incredible success, generating pride and hope for the people in his company as well as the people in the country. But Chen Lihua, one of the richest Chinese women, seems to have merely manipulated her *guanxi* (personal connections) for her enormous success in various businesses such as sandalwood manufacture and real estate. Her clever use of flattery can be demonstrated through her attitude toward foreign journalists as well. She bestowed the journalist Philip Pan with two Chinese-style padded silk jackets and a long cashmere coat that cost nearly five hundred dollars, and a thousand-dollar Hong Kong banknote; Pan refused profusely, saying that it was against the *Washington Post*'s policies, but she adamantly demanded he take the gifts, or she would take it as a

---

[13] AsiaInfo was the first private Chinese company to reach over the value of $1 billion; in fact, the company was valued at more than $5 billion. David Sheff, *China Dawn: the Story of a Technology and Business Revolution* (New York: HarperBusiness, 2002), 205.

[14] Although a conglomerate was initially solely backed by the Chinese government, Edward Tian convinced the government to allow foreign direct investment in CNC, easily raising $300 million funds and valuing the company at $2 billion. David Sheff, *China Dawn: the Story of a Technology and Business Revolution* (New York: HarperBusiness, 2002), 247.

personal insult (Pan 170-1). Chen has insisted that she earned her affluence by hard work, but when asked about the details of *how*, she merely stumbles on her words and says she would rather not say. Pan insinuates that some entrepreneurs like Chen Lihua "ingratiate the system" for success (Pan 158), and in return -- support the Communist Party.

Chen Lihua's club business also provides fun for the top party officials and earns her even more money. In order to build an extravagant club for party officials and foreign businessmen in Jinbao Avenue hutong (apartment complex), She complained and coaxed to the local party cadre and even premier Zhang to evict all the residents of the hutong. Liu Shiru, a previous homeowner of Jinbao hutong was literally thrown out of his own house and forced to accept only $800 per squared meter, while the normal price should have been $2500 per squared meter (Pan 153). About this relocation phenomenon widespread in industrializing China, the government officials allege that all the residents "relocated" are compensated fairly, and that they will be able to live in better and more modern houses. But as the article from China Daily in January 2010[15] indicates, the local government and the developers often used violence, cut electricity and water to force residents to move out. Yet, those "lucky" enough to be relocated from their tiny homes for "better" housing are often met with misfortune. Because they cannot afford the new housing, they are forced to move into a smaller housing, and often condemned to the low living that they cannot escape.

In addition to the eviction problem, inferior remuneration and working conditions also complicate the move up the social and economic ladder. In Shenzhen, where per capita is among the highest in the country, the factory girls are paid $2 a day -- "troublesome" and "less meticulous" men even less. Eight to twelve workers are crammed into a filthy and small dormitory, despite the factory's proud advertisement about its superb working conditions (Fishman 96). But because there is no

---

[15] "Owners to Get Say in Relocation." *China Daily Website - Connecting China Connecting the World.* Web. 30 Sept. 2010. <http://www.chinadaily.com.cn/china/2010-01/22/content_9359779.htm>.

workers' union independent of the Party[16], many grievances such as proper health care[17] go unaddressed. These conditions explain why labor costs so little in China. Surviving on every day basis, and unable to save any money for any enterprise, these cheap labor sources have hard time closing the income gap.

Despite its majestic GDP growth over the last several decades, China's income disparity has been only escalating. Macroeconomic policies such as establishing Special Economic Zones on the east coast and undervaluation of currency encouraged export and lowered domestic demand and income distribution. The tax revenue from rural areas, for example, was used to subsidize east coast export regions. The result was that real export as a percentage of China's GDP grew from 21% in 1998 to 57% in 2007, but China's consumption as a percentage of GDP decreased from 58% in 1970s to 35% in 2008.[18] Economist Liao Cheng thinks that government officials exploit citizens through government monopolies, widening the gap between rich and poor. Hence on a per capita basis China ranks barely above the world's poorest nations, with an average income of just over $1000 a year (Kynge 52). Ethnic minorities in the interior and western provinces such as Xinjiang have 15 times less of a income in the rural regions than the entrepreneurs (Dru 112).

---

[16] Philip Pan, *Out of Mao's Shadow: the Struggle for the Soul of a New China* (New York: Simon & Schuster, 2008), 126: Yao - Official trade union controlled by the party -- the only union allowed under the law -- rebuffed them. Mary Gallagher: "There is no effective institutional representation of either workers or employers"

[17] Philip Pan, *Out of Mao's Shadow: the Struggle for the Soul of a New China* (New York: Simon & Schuster, 2008), 115: Officials were looting their pensions and denying them proper health care. 119: "work units' had always provided housing, health care, and schools for their children, and in exchange for their service on behalf of socialism, they had been promised job security and retirement pensions. Now, suddenly they were left to fend for themselves.

[18] Jian, Tianlun. "Macroeconomic Policies Widen Income Gap in China | China | Epoch Times." *Epoch Times | National, World, China, Sports, Entertainment News | Epoch Times*. Web. 30 Sept. 2010. <http://www.theepochtimes.com/n2/content/view/28375/>

Despite its public declaration of war against income disparity, the Communist Party cadre has been the main culprit in causing the income disparity, not only with its macroeconomic policies, but also with its corruption in system. Because the party cadre will do anything to retain their power in the elite ranks, peasants are exploited in all possible ways conceivable. Qi Yuling had her *life* stolen by a classmate who had a party official as a father. From a peasantry in rural province, Qi had aced her college examination (only chance to advance her career), but was deceived that she failed the examination, when in fact, her less-deserving classmate and a party cadre's daughter had "borrowed" her name for 15 years to advance *her* career. When Qi planned to sue and demand rightful compensation, she and her family were only beaten up and silenced (Kynge 162). The examinations that are supposed to open up careers are only manipulated by the party to close the door again.

The party officials, of course, do not forget to siphon off the peasants' money and lives in conventional overtaxing schemes. The central government had issued a tax limit in 1993, especially on the poor peasants: tax could not exceed 5 percent of their income (Pan 183). Local officials often ignored this and even came up with ingenious strategems, such as the "attitude tax" for those refusing to pay the unjustified taxes (Pan 184), to collect more money to squander from the poverty-stricken peasants. Zhang Xide, who initially seemed generous and honest to Philip Pan (his book <u>Out of Mao's Shadow</u> presents overwhelming cases of corrupt and unfair China), betrayed his ugly side as Pan's research continued. Zhang crushed the peasants' outcry against unfair tax using police (Pan 189) and sued writers Chen Guidi and Wu Chuntao for "falsely defaming" him in their book *An Investigation of China's Peasantry*. The Party banned the book, but the court never issued a verdict -- caught in the dilemma between the truth and obligation to submit to party officials. In spite of his embroilment with the peasants, Zhang Xide was promoted to a higher-paying position in the nearby city of Fuyang (Pan 190).

It is even more infuriating that the money that could have saved another peasant's life only fattened the government officials' rotund stomaches. In 2003, the government officials spent $10-13 million in public money every year just on eating and drinking: a fund enough to host four Olympic games (Pan 183). [19] Furthermore, the government has frequently been "implicated in crimes that caused death," including the sale of fake baby milk powder, transfusion of HIV-contaminated blood, (Kynge 167)[20] and an abominable child-labor scheme that the government denied, in which forty-two children and teachers died in an explosion of the detonators in firecrackers third and fourth-graders were forced to install (Sheff 279-80). The extravagance of their luxurious lives contrast greatly with the moribund peasants.

The rampant corruption in the party is largely concealed or neglected by the limited civil rights and excessive propaganda, both of which restrict dissent from the mass. SARS and Tiananmen Square were two events that the Communist Party were able to belie, in order to preserve its "legitimacy" and power. Severe Acute Respiratory Syndrome killed hundreds of people around the worldwide in 2002 and 2003. CCP was integral in facilitating the spread of the epidemic because it did not let the information about SARS leak in fear that it will disrupt the flow of tourists (Pan 212), who undoubtedly provides a large source of income for the residents and the government; The government did not want to risk it. Reporters and editors who were involved in publishing any SARS story were demoted and fired; SARS was only to be reported as an "atypical pneumonia" consummately contained (Pan 215, 235). The *Southern Metropolis Daily*'s editor-in-chief Cheng Yizhong, however, decided that he could not deny the press of its rightful function: to inform the citizens of important issues. He was reprimanded and demoted for publishing a warning about SARS

---

[19] Liu Binyan (d. 2005), one of China's most prominent journalists, explicates the "Cycle of Corruption" in his essay: "The Long March from Mao: China's De-Communization." *China: Contemporary Political, Economic, and International Affairs*. Ed. Denoon, David B. H. New York: New York University Press, 2007. 80-81. Print.

[20] Page 168 describes the events' unfolding in details. James Kynge, *China Shakes the World: a Titan's Breakneck Rise and Troubled Future and the Challenge for America* (Boston: Houghton Mifflin, 2006).

(Pan 238). Soon he was bold enough to expose injustice and corruption in the shourong local detainment system (Pan 252). Wen Jiabao abolished the shourong regulations when the press and legal scholars in Beijing raged and petitioned the National People's Congress (Pan 256), but Cheng's audacity earned him five months in prison (Pan 269) and fired him from two editor-in-chief jobs (at *Southern Metropolis Daily* and *Beijing News*) he had merited (267).

The honest doctor Jiang Yanyong was also punished for "disturbing public order" (Pan 315) by exposing the dangers of SARS to the public, in defiance of the central command. Though he was known as the nation's finest surgeons (Pan 210), Jiang had become a "half-retired" doctor at his hospital because he refused to coax the Communist Party like his colleagues did. As he observed the SARS spread and kill the first several patients to die at No. 301 Hospital, Jiang sent out a letter of warning to his friends, which soon spread to foreign media at an uncontrollable pace. He was detained for warning others about the danger of SARS and revealing the more accurate number of SARS-related deaths, which the government had downplayed all along (Pan 215). When the SARS outbreak terminated, Jiang decided to chastise the government for failing to take responsibilities for the Tiananmen incident in 1989. He felt convicted of not having spoken out against the horrors of the Tiananmen Square, and described those injured from the massacre who had died in his hospital in a manuscript he sent to his friends. He was labeled as a dangerous rightist and kidnapped to be detained for seven weeks around the anniversary of Tiananmen Square incident (Pan 231-4). But Jiang wanted to meet his family, and he had to pledge to abstain from investigating and reporting. "The state had been unable to break Jiang, but it had succeeded in silencing him" (Pan 234). As the Communist Party silences bold individuals like Jiang, horrors in the past are buried underneath the CCP's version of history, understated and forgotten.

Like the Communist Party's whitewashing of its past, atrocities and suppression continue behind the international image of optimistic, growing China. Encouraging atheism and materialism, the Communist Party claims to be the top authority and persecutes anything that demonstrates potential that can

exceed the party.[21] Tibetan Buddhism, Falun Gong, and Roman
Catholicism are three of many religions that have to practice
underground. The Chinese leadership expresses disgruntlement
when foreign presidents meet Dalai Lama, as in the case of
China threatening its relations with U.S. when Obama met with
the Dalai Lama in February 2010.[22] Falun Gong, a form of
exercises for integrating mind and body for peace and harmony,
is officially banned because the group's protests showed its
incredible organizational ability that threatened the party. The
Communist Party demands total control; and hence it contends
that Tibetan Buddhism, Falun Gong, and to some extent, Roman
Catholicism, are evil cults that threaten the morals of the society.
The propaganda that hid the deadly epidemic that swept across
the globe and ignored its wrongdoings at Tiananmen continues
to defend the government and downplay mass incidents, only to
preserve its increasingly precarious power.

One useful tool that the Communist Party discovered is a
nascent nationalism among the Chinese. Propaganda in
advertisement and education ferments in the spirit of nationalism
in the heterogenous society to sustain the ramshackle society: be
proud of being *Chinese* (one thing that the Hans and the ethnic
minorities have in common). In contrast to quelling pro-
democracy or workers' protests, the Communist Party does not
suppress and sometimes even openly join the anti-foreign and
anti-Japanese protests (Kynge 216-22). Not only do the Chinese
actually despise the Japanese[23] for the Nanjing massacre, rapes,

---

[21] "No organization engaged in governance is permitted to exist
independently of the Party... Religions, too, are free to practice as long
as they accept -- at least nominally -- that the Party, which is atheist, is
a higher authority than their own spiritual leader." James Kynge, *China
Shakes the World: a Titan's Breakneck Rise and Troubled Future and
the Challenge for America* (Boston: Houghton Mifflin, 2006), 195.
[22] "China warns of 'serious damage' if Barack Obama meets Dalai
Lama."
http://www.telegraph.co.uk/news/worldnews/northamerica/usa/713636
6/China-warns-of-serious-damage-if-Barack-Obama-meets-Dalai-
Lama.html
[23] "Every schoolchild has to memorize passages of history in which
Japanese are described as 'devils' and portrayed as evil. Elementary
school students learn that the first among ten 'must-know' historical

tortures, and colonization, the anti-Japan rallies also empower the CCP by consolidating the nation under one cause. The propaganda makes it seem like CCP is effectively protecting the Chinese against the foreigners, while the CCP is calculatingly utilizing the new nationalism to integrate all of China's diverse communities (Friedman 89).

There have been predictions of China's disintegration because of its unique yet potentially explosive feature of diversity. Lucian Pye, a leading China scholar in the United States now deceased, said that "China is really a civilization pretending to be a nation-state."[24] Edward Friedman, a political science professor at University of Wisconsin, expounds on Pye's reasonable argument: "China -- like Russia, Ethiopia, and Yugoslavia -- is an empire that cannot survive growing regionalist communal identities" (Friedman 92). Once a contemporary of the Roman civilization, China has survived and retained its "Chineseness" despite its multiple dynastic changes. But like those civilizations and countries that inevitably fell apart, diversity of China may ultimately beget a collapse of the massive Tiger.

Even in Chinese history, there are many portents that parallel the downfall of the Communist Party. According to Zhou Bo from Shanghai newspaper *Wen Hui Bao*, rulers who isolated China have made China vulnerable and backward (Friedman 94)--and Communist Party fits precisely into the category of declining government. Whether China as a state becomes democratic or its parts disintegrate, the autonomous regions would benefit in various ways. Not only would they have more freedom and representation through a more democratic rule and reinforced rule of law, but also be able to use its resources (most of China's resources derive from autonomous regions) for its own advancement rather than sacrificing them to finance the east coast cities' development, leaving the rural population

---

facts is that Communist China was founded on 'one hundred years of Chinese people opposing foreign aggression'" James Kynge, *China Shakes the World: a Titan's Breakneck Rise and Troubled Future and the Challenge for America* (Boston: Houghton Mifflin, 2006), 222.

[24] Pye, Lucian W. "How China's Nationalism was Shanghaied." *Australian Journal of Chinese Affairs*. January (1993): 130. Print.

destitute and stagnant. Notwithstanding theories and physical symptoms that forecast its destruction, China's strong nationalism, whether based on fear or a unusual mix of heritage, obscures the projections of a complete fallout of the nation.

One also must remember and acclaim how much progress China *has* made in such a short period of time. The authoritative party could not destroy *all* voices of dissent: though many are repeatedly silenced and forced to forget the iniquities of the party, there are many more heroes and heroines who refuse to succumb and are martyrs for the future generations of their nation. With foreign journalists' help, dissidents are able to inform the world of China's social, economic, and environmental disintegration. Despite its frenzied attempts at covering up and making excuses, the party is gradually but certainly losing its power.

There are some other signs of progress within the borders that defy the ominous theories of China's disintegration. In addition to opposition not entirely crushed, Capitalism is dwelling (paying lip-service to "Socialism"). Environmental disasters finally began to be addressed through calculating a green GDP, using tradable permits for pollution control, and investment in clean energy (Economy 215). Foreign journalists and even China's own newspapermen are able to expose more, which leads to international criticisms and pressures for China to rectify its problems. Bo Feng of Chengwei Ventures ("Becoming" in Chinese) is in fact annoyed that many Westerners "fail to look at the complexities in China or don't acknowledge how far China has come in a very short amount of time." Feng said, "If this much is out there now, imagine what will come next? Give China time." Edward Tian, the entrepreneur already mentioned multiple times, also defended China's progress, "It has only been twenty years since China came out of the Dark Ages. It has taken the Western nations hundreds of years to develop their social and governmental systems" (Sheff 254).

China was only able to see this progress and retain hope because of many martyrs who fought for their conscience and their country (the latter, of course, is not equivalent to the CCP). Those who challenged the status quo in the face of danger brought China this far. Either by the rising dissent or by its own conscience (more like its practicality for survival), CCP itself seems to be changing slowly. One instance involves Premier Zhu Rongji apologizing for an explosion that resulted from an appalling child labor scheme by an elementary school. He had denied the report, claiming that there were no explosives kept at the school, and insisting that the explosion was "the result of a deranged man." But internet forums, chat rooms, and websites that eluded the government's vigilance continued to discuss and disseminate the story. Hence the apology: "this was seen as a breakthrough in candor."[25]

China is a formidable nation that everybody is watching. After Deng's Gaige Kaifang, CCP's opaque wrongdoings are becoming more transparent, and CCP is being watched closer. A complex mix of propaganda, force, and acquiescence seems to sustain the volatile country together. With proper changes to the political and economic structure, China could be able to accomplish a lot more than it already has. China has yet to make the greatest change. The world will be watching when the tiger takes the big flight.

---

[25] Klein, Joe. "China.org." *The New Yorker*. 23 Apr. 2001. Web. 30 Sept. 2010.
<http://www.newyorker.com/archive/2001/04/23/010423talk_comment >.

Works Cited

Economy, Elizabeth. "China's Environmental Challenge." *China: Contemporary Political, Economic, and International Affairs*. Ed. Denoon, David B. H. New York: New York University Press, 2007. 204-15. Print.

Fishman, Ted C. *China, Inc.: How the Rise of the Next Superpower Challenges America and the World*. New York: Scribner, 2005. Print.

Friedman, Edward. "China's North-South Split and the Forces of Disintegration." *China: Contemporary Political, Economic, and International Affairs*. Ed. Denoon, David B. H. New York: New York University Press, 2007. 85-95. Print.

Gladney, Dru C. "Rumblings from the Uyghur." *China: Contemporary Political, Economic, and International Affairs*. Ed. Denoon, David B. H. New York: New York University Press, 2007. 106-113. Print.

Klein, Joe. "China.org." *The New Yorker*. 23 Apr. 2001. Web. 30 Sept. 2010. <http://www.newyorker.com/archive/2001/04/23/010423talk_comment>.

Kynge, James. *China Shakes the World: a Titan's Breakneck Rise and Troubled Future and the Challenge for America*. Boston: Houghton Mifflin, 2006. Print.

Lee, Khoon Choy. *Pioneers of Modern China: Understanding the Inscrutable Chinese*. River Edge, NJ: World Scientific Pub., 2005. Print.

Liu, Binyan. "The Long March from Mao: China's De-Communization." *China: Contemporary Political, Economic, and International Affairs*. Ed. Denoon, David B. H. New York: New York University Press, 2007. 77-84. Print.

Pan, Philip P. *Out of Mao's Shadow: the Struggle for the Soul of a New China*. New York: Simon & Schuster, 2008. Print.

Pye, Lucian W. "How China's Nationalism was Shanghaied." *Australian Journal of Chinese Affairs*. January 1993. Print.

Shambaugh, David. "Sino-American Relations Since September 11: Can the New Stability Last?" *China: Contemporary Political, Economic, and International Affairs*. Ed. Denoon, David B. H. New York: New York University Press, 2007. 51-63. Print.

Sheff, David. *China Dawn: the Story of a Technology and Business Revolution*. New York: HarperBusiness, 2002. Print.

Wang, Weilan. "Making Sense of 'Mass Incidents'". *Global Times* 30 May 2009: 1.
http://special.globaltimes.cn/2009-05/433271.html

Wedeman, Andrew. "Enemies of the State: Mass Incidents and Subversion in China" (2009). APSA 2009 Toronto Meeting Paper. Available at SSRN: http://ssrn.com/abstract=1451828

Yuan, Haiwang. *This Is China: the First 5,000 Years*. Great Barrington, MA: Berkshire Pub. Group, 2010. Print.

"Preventing Heart Attacks"

Hyang Ki Lee
Tenafly High School

On Tuesday, July 13, 2010, the morning of the 2010 Major League Baseball All-Star Game, an 80-year-old man passed away from a heart attack at St. Joseph's Hospital in Tampa, Florida. The man who died nine days after his eightieth birthday was the principal owner and managing partner of Major League Baseball's New York Yankees: George Michael Steinbrenner III. Under Steinbrenner's ownership of 37 years since 1973, the Yankees thrived and proceeded with a bright future; the team earned 7 World Series titles and 11 pennants ("The New York Times Sports"). However, even this influential and honorable man could not avoid the vicious and unwelcomed visitor that knocked at his door; the bane of Steinbrenner's death was heart attack. Although Steinbrenner failed to overcome the baneful disease (possibly because of his old age), studies and efforts of many concerned doctors have produced ways to prevent the heart attack (Chung 19).

When people are asked about the location of the heart, they either do not know or know the wrong information; most say that it is located in the left chest. Why? Because left is where they feel heart beats. While it is true that heart beats stronger on the left side of the chest, it is incorrect to assume that the heart is located on the left side. The heart is not located on either side of chest; it is in the center between the two lungs (Agatston 16, Chung 2, Rippe 16). It is plausible that people think the heart is located on the left side because the heart, in fact, is slightly slanted to the left side.

20

Most people are disinterested about their hearts because a heart is an invisible and automatic muscle that never rests. But, what if the organ that seems trivial suddenly malfunctions or even discontinues? "Worldwide, twenty-three people each minute have a heart attack. This adds up to about 12 million heart attacks a year" (Berra 3). Heart attack is the number one killer in America with one out of five deaths each year; that is more than 50% of all deaths. "Nearly 1.5 million individuals suffer an acute heart attack every year in the United States alone. That's about one individual every 20 seconds. Worse yet, one-third of them die, and about one-half of these deaths occur within an hour of the event and usually are a result of cardiac rhythm problems associated with the heart attack" (Rippe 61). However, with efforts from many passionate cardiologists, this fatal and dreaded disease can be prevented with modern treatments.

Before going into the topic, it is essential to know about the structure and the role of a heart. A heart is a four-chambered muscle, composed of millions of hardworking cells, that is located between rib cages. It is protected by rib cages, muscles, and other structures of the chest wall. The heart is composed of a pumping muscle called the myocardium, surrounded by a tough and protective membrane called pericardium, the only kind in the body. The heart muscle is unique and differs from any other muscles in the body because it does not rest; it cannot survive a moment without sufficient amount of oxygenated blood, while the other muscles can perform briefly without the deliverance of oxygen. The fist-sized organ serves a critical and vital purpose in the body by pumping the blood and delivering oxygen and nutrients essential for the cells throughout the body (Chung 3, Myers 1, Rippe 16).

Each side of the heart, left and right, contains an atrium and a ventricle. Ventricles, which are situated below atria (plural form of atrium), are separated by a thick muscular wall called the ventricular septum. The main function of ventricles is to pump blood to the lungs or to the body. The atria, separated by the muscular wall named atrial septum, are located above the ventricles and mainly serve to receive blood from the lungs and the entire body, and to push the blood down to the ventricles (Agatson 16, Chung 2-5, Myers 1-2, Rippe 15-16, Wilde 300).

21

"From a cardiologist's point of view, it is the left ventricle that is the most important chamber because it is the area of the heart most likely to be affect by a heart attack" (Agatston 17). And it is true, since the most heart diseases are focused on that area (Agatston 17).

The cardiovascular system or circulatory system, including the heart, blood, and blood vessels, is not as complex as it seems. The double-looped system is very efficient in supplying the blood to all the living cells in the body and sending back the used up blood back to the heart to be resupplied with oxygen. The first loop is between the heart and the lungs and the second loop is between the heart and the entire body. The flow of blood in and out of the heart and from chamber to chamber is regulated by four valves: the mitral, aortic, tricuspid, and pulmonic valves, which make sure that the blood flows in one direction and prevent back-flow. From the heart, blood is pumped away to the body through arteries and returns to the heart through veins. Deoxygenated blood from the body and head enters right atrium through veins called superior and inferior vena cava. Then, the blood passes through tricuspid valve into the right ventricle, which pumps the blood out the pulmonary valve to the lungs, where the blood gives away carbon dioxide and receives a new supply of oxygen. The oxygen-rich blood returns to the heart and enters the left atrium. Then it passes through the mitral valve into the left ventricle. The left ventricle contracts to pump the oxygenated blood out the aortic valve, and the blood is distributed throughout the body via the aorta, the main artery of the body (Agatston 17, Chung 5-6, Myers 1-2, Rippe 17-18, 22, Wilde 299).

While it contracts and pumps out the blood to supply every cells in the body with oxygen and nutrients, the heart itself has to receive oxygen and necessary nutrients. The heart receives its aliments through its own vessels called coronary arteries. Just like any other arteries that deliver oxygenated blood to parts of the body, coronary arteries also branch off from the aorta. The heart does not absorb its needs directly from the blood in its chambers, but has to pump out and deliver the blood itself through the arteries as to any other parts in the body. From the aorta, two main trunks of coronary arteries, the right coronary artery (RCA) and the left main coronary artery, stretch down the heart. The left main coronary artery branches into the circumflex (LCX), which circles around the side of the heart, and the left anterior descending artery (LAD), which runs down the front of the heart (Myers 3). Because the coronary arteries supply oxygen-rich blood to the heart muscle called myocardium, any occlusion to these three main coronary arteries, RCA, LCX, and LAD, will bring about heart failures (Agatston 17, Chung 12-13, Rippe 19, 62).

The most common form of heart disease is coronary artery disease (CAD) or atherosclerosis (Rippe 29). As its name implies, coronary artery disease is an aberration of coronary arteries. The coronary artery has a diameter of about 2 to 3 mm, which is fairly narrow for the heart to depend its survival on. When these coronary arteries are narrowed, causing the heart to receive inadequate blood supply, the process is called coronary artery disease (Chung 13). When the hardening and the narrowing (stenosis) of the arteries advance, the victims begin to experience chest pain called angina, which is the warning for the heart attack (Chung 14). When the coronary artery stenosis exacerbates, one or more coronary arteries may get completely clogged (Rippe 17, 19). The coronary artery disease is fatal to the heart because heart cannot survive without the supplies of blood; narrowing of the coronary arteries hinders the heart from getting its resources (Rippe 17). Because the heart is the center of life, its failing to deliver the supplies not only endangers itself, but also imperils the entire body.

So, how are the coronary artery disease and the heart attack related? "Heart attack is the most severe result of CAD" (Rippe 15). In terms of the CAD, angina is the moderate result and heart attack is the severe one. "It's the difference between squeezing through a partially shut door and being locked out" (Myers 61). The victims of CAD experience angina when the artery is partially closed, and experience heart attack when the artery is severely or completely blocked. Heart attack, known medically as myocardial infarction (MI), occurs when one of more of the three main coronary arteries become completely blocked, causing dead heart muscles (Berra 4, Chung 14, 18-19, *Harvard Heart Letter* 1, Myers 61, Rippe 61-62). "If anything obstructs the flow of blood through one of these arteries (coronary arteries) for more than 20-30 min, the heart will likely not receive enough oxygen, and the part of the heart muscle fed by that artery will die" (Agatston 17). As described by Agatston, during a heart attack, the zenith of the coronary artery disease, the part of the heart that does not receive the blood dies and will not recover easily.

According to Agatston, the author of the *New York Times* Bestseller *The South Beach Diet*,"Heart Failure occurs when a heart muscle is damaged to the point that the heart can no longer pump sufficient blood to the rest of the organs." 89%-90% of heart attack and strokes are caused by blood clots (Wilde 334). Blood clots form by inflammation, which is "the body's reaction to nearly all injuries" (Myers 56). Before the cardiologists uncovered the real causes of the heart attack, the early pathologists thought that a blood clot formed when a yellow and waxy substance, called plaque, builds up inside a coronary artery, gradually blocking and stagnating the blood flow, the process they named *arteriosclerosis* (*atherosclerosis* in modern form), the *"hardening of the arteries"* in Latin (Agatson 17-18, Rippe 240). In other words, the early investigators from more than a century ago assumed that the blood clot is not the cause of blocking the blood flow, but rather, the aftermath that is caused by the plaque's blocking the flow; their surmise was wrong (Agatston 18-19). Dr. Russel Ross, who is referred to as the *"founder of contemporary vascular biology,"* was first to recognize that "atherosclerosis is actually the result of an inflammatory one," which is "a concept contrary to the theory that had been previously accepted as gospel," according to a report from the *American Heart Association* (Wilde 67-68).

What the early investigators missed was that the plaque itself does not block the blood flow. To begin with, there are two types of plaques, soft and hard. It is the soft or unstable plaque that causes the problem while the hard and stable plaque is easily healed; most often, it is the rupturing of the soft plaque that causes a heart attack. Arthur Agatston makes an analogy with the process by saying, "the best way to picture a soft plaque is to think of it as a small 'pimple' protruding from underneath the delicate inner lining of the artery called endothelium." Filled with cholesterol, the soft plaque may burst open, "puncturing a hole in the endothelium and exposing the contents of the soft plaque to the bloodstream" (Agatston 19). Thus, the explosion of the soft plaque, not the plaque itself, instigates the blood to cluster around the wound and block the blood flow.

The procedure that is executed in the body until the actual plaque forms and ruptures is very intriguing, but complex and dangerous. The endothelial cells that line the wall of coronary arteries absorb nutrients while aiding the blood-flow. However, along with good and healthful nutrients that enter through the lining cells, bad cholesterol called LDL (low-density lipoprotein) cholesterol seeps through the cells and sets into a layer beneath them called the sub endothelial layer. After its adherence to the artery lining, the LDL cholesterol is attacked by a substance called a free radical, which causes the chemical reaction called oxidation. Possibly the most dangerous chemical reaction in human body, oxidation instigates the release of cytokines, intracellular chemicals that are very small and act like "poison daggers." The cytokines triggered by oxidation begin to create blockages called atherosclerotic plaques in the arteries. Then, oxidation's next job is to disguise the LDL's identity so the immune system can no longer recognize it. Once the LDL becomes incognito, inflammation, which is the body's reaction to and defense against injuries and infection, takes place. Inflammation "recruits immune system repair and fighter cells," and the recruits of immune system start attacking the "unknown substance" in the body (Myers 56, Rippe 45). During the attack, the white blood cells called macrophages engorge the LDL and perish by self-destruction. As they engulf the LDL, the macrophages transform into macrophage foam cells, which resemble yellow fatty streaks that abide in the center of the plaque. The soft and squishy plaque continuously swells up and grows larger until it explodes like a firework; the fatal rupture occurs when a substance called metalloproteinase breaks open the cap of the plaque, causing its vulnerability and volatility. While metalloproteinase works its way outward, the pressure of blood-flow works it was inward, pushing around the plaque, and eventually fracturing the weary plague (Arnot 18-20,23,24, Rippe 47).

When the plaque fractures, as mentioned above, the consequence is fatal and ugly; the chance of dying is one in four. This unpleasant and complex explosion is not the 'main cause' of heart attack, but it certainly is an accident that eventually leads to heart attack. After the explosion, the walls of the artery are injured, and blood clot forms at the injured hole to clog and heal the site. This clot is what causes obstruction of blood flow, making the arteries of heart attack victims hard and inflexible. As it turns out, the clot is not the result of atherosclerosis, hardening of the arteries due to the occlusion of blood flow by the plaque as the early medical investigators had surmised; it is the cause (Agatston 8-9, 18-19, Wilde 25, 67-74).

The discovery about the real cause of atherosclerosis is very crucial because the knowledge about the blood clot provided a fundamental key to understand the "mechanism of a heart attack" that enables the victims to prevent and treat heart disease (Agatson 19). Heart attack, however, would not be on a hot topic list if it is only affected by the plaque and the blood clot. Heart disease is much more complex than what the last decades have witnessed: "Real cause of a heart attack is different from what is commonly believed" (Agatston 18). The source for real cause of heart attack was ameliorated by researchers and cardiologists who have refuted the antecedent belief of the cause of atherosclerosis, such as Dr. Ross. Doctors discover more risk factors for CAD from long-term studies such as the Framingham Study, which included 10,000 men and women for more than 50 years (Rippe 30). Furthermore, many hidden factors and causes that were dismissed or invisible are now unveiled and discovered and are added to amend the diagnostic systems along with the common factors that are widely known to even children.

The common risk factors that increase the rate of heart attack are family history, old age, gender, smoking, high blood cholesterol, high blood pressure or hypertension, diabetes, and obesity, according to many doctors such as Karol Watson, Bob Arnot, James Rippe and numerous doctors in the world. "A risk factor is a personal habit, practice, or physical characteristic or condition that increases the likelihood that people develop CAD" (Rippe 30). Obviously, nothing can be done with old age and family inheritance, but the rest can be controlled and reduced.

Besides the common factors that are mentioned, there are many abstruse factors that were recently discovered or still need world-wide attention to be analyzed, such as the blood clotting, c-reactive protein (CRP), Lp(a), homocysteine, and other factors (Myers 35). Those factors will not be covered in depth on account of their perplexity and vastness, but the glimpses of their basic ideas will be mentioned. Keep in mind that however complex or obscure the factors are, the modern science has already discovered or is able to ascertain the proper treatment.

If a person has an inheritance of heart disease, meaning the disease is carried in the genes and has been passed on from generation to generation, his or her close relatives probably have had heart attacks and passed away already, and the person, too, is likely exposed to the CAD. In that case, it is mandatory to get an advanced diagnostic blood testing to find out whether he or she has good, bad, or terrible cholesterol-carrying particles or other dangerous substances such as C-reactive protein, "a marker for inflammation that can damage the lining of arteries" (Agatston 41). The cholesterol-carrying particle increases the rate of occlusion in the arteries (as illustrated before), which develops into blood clots that has to be treated immediately. There is no precaution for the people with the inheritance since the disease is congenital, but they undoubtedly can prevent any further progressions of the disease.

Along with the family inheritance, old age and gender are the risk factors of heart disease that cannot be modified. It is not surprising that a person over the age of 65 has a heart risk greater than that of younger people. As adduced in the intro, George Steinbrenner's heart attack was probably prompted by his old age. Because elder's heart has had to work longer, the artery walls are wearier and have accumulated more plaques (Agatston 52-53, Wilde 32-36, 76-78). Now, men are more likely to be exposed to CAD than woman. For men who are older than 45 and for women who are older than 55, age is a significant risk factor for CAD. However, this unfair and sexist principle comes to an end after a certain age; men and women have approximately the same risk for CAD after age 65 (Rippe 37).

The risk factors are very dangerous because their effects on CAD do not add up, but multiply. According to a data from the Framingham Heart Study, when individuals are exposed to a single risk factor, their chances of developing heart disease double up. Individuals with two risk factors have quadruple chances, and three risk factors have increased chances of 8 to 20 times (Rippe 31). In the case of a smoker, the risk of heart disease increases by double because smoking narrows the arteries, raises the blood pressure and increases the risk of irregular heartbeat, and makes the blood viscous. Smoking is the number one risk factor and the "leading cause of premature death in the United States each year, claiming more than 400,000 lives" (Rippe 34). Smoking also lowers HDL (high-density lipoprotein), which is good cholesterol, and increases inflammation, which damages the arteries (Berra 6-7, Rippe 34-35, Wilde 51, 76-78, 244-250). Smoking is "a recipe for a heart attack. There is a good reason that cigarettes are called 'coffin nails'" (Agatston 44). The good news is, according to the US Surgeon General, the risk of heart disease begins to decline as soon as a person stops smoking; smoking is the factor that can be modified (Agatston 45).

High blood cholesterol is also a preventable factor that can be modified. Cholesterol is a soft, fat-like lipid that is found in the cell membranes. Mostly produced in the liver, cholesterol is vital to body structure and function. Cholesterol is not only essential to the structure and function of body cells, but also vital to body for forming certain hormone, which regulate the body system, and bile acids, which aid in digesting. Cholesterol travels via blood streams, but since it cannot be dissolved in the blood, it needs carriers called lipoproteins for transportation. There are two major carriers: low-density lipoprotein (LDL) and high-density lipoprotein (HDL). LDL, referred to as "bad dump truck," carries cholesterol and dumps its load into the arteries, including the coronary arteries. Accumulated on the walls of the arteries, LDL generates inflammation, causing atherosclerosis, which then leads to angina and heart attacks. On the other hand, HDL picks up the cholesterol from the walls of the arteries and carries it back to the liver, where it is transformed into bile acids for aiding digestion. Although cholesterol is integral to the body, only small amount is needed to maintain a healthy life (Chung 27, Myers 22-23). "People with high levels of the good cholesterol (HDL) and low levels of bad cholesterol (LDL) have the lowest incidence of coronary artery disease (CAD)" (Myers 23).

High blood pressure damages the heart because too much blood pressure within the arteries may abrade the walls of the arteries, stimulating inflammation, which eventually leads to heart attacks (Chung 15). "Landmark studies conducted in the 1960s put to rest any serious doubt that elevated blood pressure, or *hypertension* (abnormally elevated blood pressure), represents a substantial risk for developing CAD and stroke. Hypertension is extremely common in the United States, probably because of the nutritional habits, propensity to gain weight, and sedentary lifestyle of most Americans" (Rippe 33). Since high blood pressure is a modified factor, "lowering blood pressure to normal will dramatically decrease the chances of having a heart attack or stroke" (Myers 10).

Diabetes mellitus is not only the factor that accelerates the risk of heart attack, but also the cause of many other diseases. Heavy meals and inactivity produced a shocking number of people with diabetes in America, putting tens of millions of people at high risk for heart disease. About 70% of people under heart disease treatment either have prediabetes or diabetes. "Diabetes is well known as a disease characterized by the body's inability to process sugars and starches. Less well known are the problems that people with diabetes have processing fats in their diet," which leads to "low levels of good HDL and elevated levels of triglycerides" (Agatston 46). Diabetes also elevates the levels of LDL, the bad cholesterol, which is considered a bad combination with the low level of HDL. In order to prevent the fatal result, people with diabetes should keep their blood pressure down and eliminate baked goods, snack food, and other starchy and sugary food from their diet (Agatston 46-47, Myers 29, Rippe 37, Wilde 251-256). It is highly recommended that they exercise, lose weight, and change diet in order to lower the risk because "Diabetes is a controllable disease" only if the patients become involved in simple health style modifications including diet and exercise, and monitor their risk factors regularly (Wilde 255).

Diabetes is interrelated with obesity; in fact, "many overweight people have other risk factors, such as high blood pressure, abnormal blood cholesterol, diabetes, etc. By definition, obesity means 30% extra weight, and about 60% of American people are obese" (Chung 33). Obesity increases blood pressure, blood cholesterol levels, and diabetes. It also elevates LDL cholesterol levels and other fats in the blood, which cause formation of plaques, while lowering HDL cholesterol levels (Rippe 36). "Most people find that losing weight is very difficult. The benefits are enormous, though, especially if the weight is carried in the waist, so that they are shaped like an apple rather than a pear" (Berra 13). A 2005 Israeli study, which involved more than 1,000 men, reported that "those with large bellies were 1.5 times more likely to die from a stroke than men with a more even distribution of fat" (Agatston 50). Obesity is the risk factor of CAD that attracts other risk factors, thereby accelerating the development of CAD even more.

Besides the common risk factors that are well known to the world, there are "undetected" and "unrealized" risk factors that threaten people. Many people who were informed to have perfect health conditions by their doctors actually have had heart attacks. Why is that so? Is there a hidden factor that triggers heart attacks? The answer is yes. The average cholesterol level, which is combined levels of LDL and HDL, among patients admitted to the hospital suffering a heart attack was not 240 as most people expect, but actually was 220. Today, it is recommended that the patients reach 150 total cholesterol after they have had heart attacks. Why not then, the number 150 recommended prior to the heart attack? Many doctors dismiss the new information by saying, "All you need to do is eat three good meals a day and exercise." According to Dr. Antonio Gotto, Dean of Cornell Medical College, "Even if your LDL or so called 'bad' cholesterol is considered average, you may still be at risk if your HDL, or 'good' cholesterol is too low" (Wilde 41). Many precarious doctors fail to diagnose not only the safe cholesterol level, but also the blood pressure and many other factors that endanger their patients.

Although the doctors' conservatism appears to be a threat to many patients, there are many other risk factors that are recently discovered such as the blood clot and analyzed to amend the obsolete and outdated diagnosis. These risks include homocysteine, C-reactive protein, Lp(a), and other factors. Homocysteine is an amino acid that is "considered to create an increased risk for coronary artery disease and stroke" and "may harm the lining of the arteries and contribute to blood clotting" (Chung 24). C-reactive protein, a marker that increases as an indicator of the inflammation, was "first discovered in 1931 by Oswald Theodore Avery" (Myers 37). "C-reactive protein (CRP) recently received special attention because CRP is shown to be one of the important coronary risk factors" (Chung 25). Lp(a) is a lipoprotein that is similar to LDL (Rippe 40). Lp contains cholesterol and "promote blood clotting, thus increasing the chance of a heart attack" (Myers 36).

As discussed and uncovered earlier, every factors that risks heart attack can be diagnosed and prevented with treatments. "The past thirty years have shown a dramatic decline in mortality rates from heart disease. Between 1975 and 1995 (the date of the last available statistics), the mortality rate within the first thirty days after a heart attack dropped 63 percent" (Myers intro). In addition, "the death rate from heart attacks decreased by about 25 percent during the last decade, and recent studies show that heart attacks are being diagnosed earlier and treated more effectively than ever before. And there's plenty of room for doctors to do even better" (Rippe 61). Heart attacks are constantly knocking on people's doors, but more and more people are learning to turn the ferocious visitors away.

Even if a person has an inherited disease or has aged, the danger of heart attack can be significantly reduced by not having any other factors that trigger heart attack. Remember, the worst and the most fatal risk is when more than one or even all the factors are combined. Therefore, it is individual's responsibility to engage in at least 30 minutes of exercise a day, choose healthy diet, reduce stress, and check up with a doctor regularly (Agatston 175, 182, *Harvard Heart Letter* 2, Rippe 124). Doing so would involve changing his or her life dramatically, but think about the extended lifespan he or she would enjoy!

It is highly recommended that a person with a heart disease ingest at least two fish meals a week. "Certain types of seafood, especially in oily, deepwater fish such as tuna, rainbow and lake trout, salmon, herring, sardine, and Spanish mackerel" contain "good fats" that are helpful for healthy heart (Agatston 58). Instead of fast foods and fatty meat, a plate should be filled with lots of fresh fruits, vegetables, and unprocessed grains that contain compounds that help protect a body from many diseases, including heart disease. What should be avoid are "refined, processed carbohydrates, including many commercially baked breads, cookies, chips, crackers, and other snack foods that may contain trans fats" (Agatson 59). It is also proven that consuming red wine daily, about 5-ounce glasses, has favorable effects in raising HDL. Also, studies show that dark chocolate helps enhance the blood flow and lower blood pressure. All those aliments mentioned above are efficient in lowering LDL while raising HDL and sustaining a healthy heart (Agatston 141-165, Chung 31, 130-132, Rippe 32).

While it is very essential to prevent and treat heart attack, it is also crucial to identify and comprehend the signals sent by hearts before the damage is irreparable: Do not underestimate or dismiss premonitory symptoms. People need to work on their "foresights" because "about two-thirds of the individuals who experience an acute heart attack also experience some warning symptoms in the weeks or days preceding the acute event. They often don't realize what the warning signs were until after the event" (Rippe 63). Dr. Jeffrey Borer, Dr. Thomas Graboys, and Dr. Claude Lenfant emphasize the importance of taking the symptoms seriously. Dr. Arnot states that "discomfort or abnormal sensation in chest area, indigestion, difficulty in breathing, feeling faint, light-headedness, palpitations, and unusual tiredness are all symptoms of the heart disease" (Arnot 46-47).

Indigestion is one of the abstract symptoms because it is very hard to distinguish from reflux disease, a disease with agonizing pain, in which some reflux of the stomach's acid flows up into the esophagus and burns the wall. Therefore, pains or abnormalities of digestion system caused by heart disease and reflux disease are almost indistinguishable; often, many patients have both diseases, so it is hard to tell which disease is causing the discomfort (Arnot 47, Rippe 53). Dr. James Atkins of the University of Texas Southern Medical Center says, "That's why we miss heart attacks in the emergency department at times, because the symptoms sound more like reflux disease" (Arnot 47).

Unlike indigestion, a symptom that is both caused by heart disease and reflux disease, fatigue is very reliable and a common symptom. Fatigue is an unusual tiredness that comes with exertion. In a study of people who faced sudden deaths, the most common symptom was fatigue. Furthermore, in accord with Dr. Borer and Dr. Lenfant who put an emphasis on the importance of fatigue, Dr. Thomas Graboys from Harvard states that "The most common symptom that my patients talk to me about is their fatigue" (Arnot 48). He also confirms that when patients experience any symptoms such as throat, jaw, chest, neck or arm discomfort in extremely cold or humid ambient during an exercise, he has no choice but to conclude that they have heart problems (Arnot 48-49, Myers 63). When people have such new sensation of exertion, they should definitely talk to doctors about it. Especially for women, fatigue is a key and crucial symptom: a recent study of women showed that 95% of women with heart diseases experienced fatigue a month before their heart attacks (Arnot 48-49).

Many people are familiarized with the heart attacks mimicked by the Hollywood actors, who suddenly gasp, grasp, and collapse with startled expressions. However, heart attacks are not necessarily associated with chest sensations that are stabbing and agonizing. Arnot states that "Most of the cardiologists I spoke to agree that any abnormal sensation in the region of the chest is a potential indicator that something is going on," not necessarily a pain. The typical chest sensation will be an exertion in the middle of the chest, but any symptom within some range around the chest should not be taken lightheartedly. Unlike Dr. Thomas Graboys who confirms that fatigue is the most common symptom his patients experience, the Framingham Study found chest discomfort the most common symptom through forty years of research. Chest discomfort is not really a pain; it is just abnormal and unusual sensations that are "boring and dull." The sensations are not writhing pain; they are gradual and insidious, addling the patients, and come and go. Because victims of heart attacks usually don't experience writhing and agonizing pain, they may think the chest sensations are trivial and merely dismiss them. Because "Hollywood heart attacks" do not really happen, according to Dr. James Atkin, people have wrong assumptions about the symptoms and simply underestimate the "real" symptoms. Also, people dismiss the case, especially in case of women, because many patients have no chest sensations or discomforts at all; 43% of women have no chest symptoms and heart attacks are missed more in women (Arnot 49-51, Chung 41-42).

Heart is the center of human's rhythmic life; without it, every single cell in a body ceases to live. The heart is so intricate, but tiny for its tremendous responsibility; it is amazing that the heart endures all the pressure and overloads of work on its shoulders. The indispensable organ is risked by so many known and unknown factors that undermine its essence and purpose. From inherited risks to adopted risks, the heart is being pressured by unnecessary stress that could be diagnosed and prevented. It is then, an individual's responsibility to reduce the number of deaths caused by heart attack in America by getting involved in exercise, healthy diet, losing weight, quitting smoke, and most importantly, enjoying daily life. The earlier the procedure is followed, the better it is! Heart disease prevention, "must begin in early childhood or adolescence" (Wilde 58). Although Steinbrenner's generation was uninformed and unaware of the risk factors and the precautions, this generation and the upcoming generations are hopefully more aware of their hearts because "you do not have to experience a heart attack or stroke! They are preventable!" (Agatston 40).

Bibliography

Agatston, Arthur. *The South Beach Heart Program: the 4-step Plan That Can save Your Life*. [Emmaus, Pa.]: Rodale, 2007. Print.

Arnot, Robert Burns. *Seven Steps to Stop a Heart Attack*. New York: Simon & Schuster, 2005. Print.

Berra, Kathy. *Heart Attack!: Advice for Patients by Patients*. New Haven: Yale UP, 2002. Print.

Chung, Edward K. *100 Questions & Answers About Heart Attack and Related Cardiac Problems*. Sudbury, MA: Jones and Bartlett, 2004. Print.

"Heart attacks come in all kinds, sizes. (Cover story)." *Harvard Heart Letter* 21.1 (2010): 1-2.

Academic Search Premier. EBSCO. Web. 16 Aug. 2010.

Rippe, James M. *Heart Disease for Dummies*. Hoboken, NJ: Wiley, 2004. Print.

"The New York Times Sports." Review. *George Steinbrenner, Who Built Yankees Into Powerhouse, Dies at 80* 13 July 2010: 1-3. *The New York Times - Breaking News, World News & Multimedia*. 13 July 2010. Web. 31 Aug. 2010. <http://www.nytimes.com/2010/07/14/sports/baseball/14 steinbrenner.html>.

Wilde, Christian. *Hidden Causes of Heart Attack and Stroke: Inflammation, Cardiology's New Frontier*. Valley Village, CA: Abigon, 2003. Print.

"The Great Steel Strike of 1919"

James DongHwi Kim
Clarkstown North High School

The early part of the 20th Century was a time of chaos and change for the world and especially for the United States in terms of labor unions. When World War I ended on November 11th, 1918,[1] President Wilson shifted his attention towards building strong international relations through such means as the League of Nations and, in effect, neglected domestic labor disputes. Thus, the United States federal government under President Wilson neglected needed arbitration between labor unions and corporations in the postwar period. This led to labor unions rising up in protest against major United States corporations, creating social unrest. This is particularly evident in the "Great Steel Strike of 1919." It was declining working conditions, such as low wages coupled with long working hours, which propelled the Amalgamated Association of Iron and Steel Workers (AA) to launch a nationwide strike against the United States Steel Corporation, headed by Chairman Elbert H. Gary, on September 22, 1919.[2] The Steel Strike of 1919 mobilized more than 300,000 workers into walking out from their workplaces, such as in Pueblo, Colorado, or other cities like Chicago, Illinois.[3] The strike ended in a dismal failure due to many factors, such as the Red Scare, the inflation, and the lack of government support.

---

[1] Dubofsky, Melvyn. *Hard Work The Making of Labor History.* Chicago: University of Illinois Press, 2000.
[2] Bimba, Anthony. *The History of The American Working Class.* New York: International Publishers Co., INC., 1927. Pg 274
[3] Robert K. Murray. "Communism and the Great Steel Strike of 1919" *The Mississippi Valley Historical Review,* Vol. 38, No. 3. (Dec., 1951), pp. 445-466. JSTOR

The Amalgamated Association of Iron and Steel Workers was one of the most recognizable unions in the late 19th century and the early 20th century. More commonly known as the AA, the labor union was formed in 1876. The union was a formation of three labor unions, which were the Sons of Vulcan, Iron Steel Heaters Union, and the Iron and Steel Roll Hands Union. The main object of the AA was the "elevation of its members, the maintenance of their best interests, and to obtain, by conciliation or by other means that are just and legal, a fair remuneration to its members for their labor."[4] The union was successful in meeting the objectives it set for itself from 1876 to 1892.

However, in 1892 the Homestead Strike signified the turning point of Amalgamated Association of Iron and Steel Workers' (AA) success and the strike of 1901 further weakened the union.[5] The Homestead Strike of 1892 was held against Carnegie Steel Company in Homestead, Pennsylvania in 1892. But as conflicts arose between the workers and the pinkertons, both sides started firing at one another. This conflict resulted in the death of three pinkertons and seven workers.[6] As people died the labor union received the pointing finger, losing the support of the public. It led to the failure of the strike and the weakening and decline of membership in the union. Then the AA organized another strike in 1901 in order to receive recognition of their labor union. Their opponent was the American Sheet Steel. But the strike also ended in failure as the company brought in strikebreakers in order to take up the missing spot of the workers who were on strike.[7] The turning point for the AA was the Homestead Strike of 1892, where the failure of the strike resulted in the decline of the union in membership and support. Thereafter the decline was not able to

---

[4] Wright, Carroll D. JSTOR.
http://www.jstor.org/pss/1882283?cookieSet=1.
[5] Burgoyne, Arthur G. *Homestead*. Pittsburgh: Harvard College Library, 1893.
[6] Krause, Paul, *The Battle for Homestead, 1880-1892: Politics, Culture, and Steel*. University of Pittsburgh Press, 1992
[7] Brody, David, *Steelworkers in America: The Nonunion Era*. Harper & Row, 1969

be reversed, although slowed and somewhat restored during WWI.

The early 20th Century was a time of war. When the Archduke Franz Ferdinand of Austria was assassinated on June 28 1914,[8] it caused a chain reaction by which eventually all the nations were at war, in what was known as the Great War or more commonly as WWI. The end of the war in 1918 had direct impact on U.S. economy. One effect was the inflation into which the U.S. economy dived. One of the causes were that as the war ended, the demand for U.S. goods such as food or war materials disappeared, and as demand declined and production inclined, U.S. economy was led into inflation. Also, as war veterans came back, they needed places to work, causing many to be unemployed. Unemployment was the case for many women as companies hired back men and laid off women who had sustained these companies during the war. The bad economic condition certainly led to the failure of the Steel Strike of 1919.

However, the most influential cause from the war that contributed in the failure of the Steel Strike of 1919 was the Red Scare. The Red Scare was a product of the Bolshevik Revolution in Russia in 1917[9] and was also a product of WWI, as the U.S. sympathized with non-communist countries. The Bolshevik Revolution showed the Americans how communists were able to take over a country and set it up as a communist nation. This then installed fear into the hearts of Americans that communists were within the U.S. and were plotting to undermine the country. This idea threw the U.S. people into a state of panic.

The Red Scare during the early 1900's was the first of the two that resulted in U.S. history so far. The first Red Scare being caused by the rise of socialists in Europe and the successful Bolshevik Revolution in Europe had a significant impact on the U.S.. The American public being caught up in the national hysteria of fearing communism randomly started pointing fingers and accused people of being communists. New immigrants that were arriving at the time, especially from

---

[8] "See Serb Plot in Royal Murders." *New York Times*, 30 June 1914

[9] Dubofsky, Melvyn. *Hard Work The Making of Labor History*. Chicago: University of Illinois Press, 2000

Eastern Europe, were the ones who were under the most suspicion. Among the people who accused others, one who stood out was A. Mitchell Palmer, President Woodrow Wilson's Attorney General. Palmer, having received bomb threats and barely escaping death with his family when an anarchist planted a bomb on his porch, set his mind on attacking the source of the violence. Palmer believing that radicalism was the source of all this violence, and being "convinced that revolutionary upheaval was imminent,"[10] launched raids on these radicals and anarchists such as his raid on an anarchist group in Buffalo on July 1919.[11] But Palmer officially started these raids on radicalism when on November 1919 he launched his campaign against radicalism. The Great Steel Strike of 1919 being in the midst of this campaign fell under the category of being a conspiracy of the aliens which meant that it was a plan by radicals and communists to unsettle the U.S.. Not only was the Steel Strike of 1919 seen as an act of communism but any unrest such as strikes that resulted, were put down by the government as federal troops helped break the strike.

There were many factors why the steel workers chose to strike on the September of 1919. The first and foremost reason was the disbandment of the National War Labor Board (NWLB). The National War Labor Board was set up by Woodrow Wilson in 1918 in order to insure that the productivity during the war was reliable. So, the main purpose of the NWLB was to arbitrate the disputes and conflict between the workers and the employers and make productivity as efficient as possible without any problems from the relationship between the workers and the employers.[12] But when the war ended, the NWLB was also disbanded. With the disbandment of the board, the concern for labor unions by the government declined and was put aside.[13] Advising Wilson regarding how to deal with the labor unions was Joseph Tumulty, President Woodrow Wilson's Secretary.

---

[10] Zieger, Robert H., and Gilbert J. Gall. *American Workers, American Unions*. Baltimore: The Johns Hopkins University Press, 2002
[11] Ibid.
[12] The National Archives. http://www.archives.gov/research/guide-fed-records/groups/002.html (April 2, 2010)
[13] Ibid.

Tumulty contributed to the cause of the strike as he did not favor labor unions. He stated to Palmer that "The country at large would think that we are making a special appeal to labor at this time. If there is any class in this country to which we have been overgenerous it has been labor. I think that this class owes us more than they have been willing to give."[14] Wilson's administration, being filled with people such as Palmer and Tumulty, deserted their relations with the labor unions and their activities. While Wilson was focused mainly on the postwar affairs, he ignored the appeals of the labor unions such as the American Federation of Labor (AFL). With the absence of the NWLB to settle the conflicts between the workers and employers and the uncaring attitude of the government toward the unions and the workers, employers started to take advantage of the workers, pushing them back. This resulted in low wages, long work hours, and the inability to use collective bargaining. Ultimately, this led to the strike as these factors provoked the workers and unions to take action.

The method of going on strikes was to basically force the employers or the companies to come into terms with the workers by refusing to work and therefore making the employers or companies lose money. But the Steel Strike of 1919 failed in this case because although a huge number of workers walked out, such as 300,000 workers, even more number were unemployed and were willing to work and take the place of these strikers. These strikebreakers weakened the effect of the Steel Strike of 1919 had on the U.S. Steel Corporation. Then, on top of this, new waves of immigrants looking for jobs further threatened the positions the strikers were in by taking their jobs.

Looking at causes for the Steel Strike of 1919, one has to note also that union leaders played a large role in the direction the unions headed, which ultimately led to the Steel Strike of 1919. One leader was William Z. Foster who proposed a resolution to the Chicago Federation of Labor on April 7, 1918.[15] The resolution was to hold a meeting among all the national and

---

[14] A. Mitcheel Palmer to the Chamber of Commerce, Moberly, Missouri, Dec. 1, 1919, Department of Labor, Joe Tumulty, 148-149
[15] Bimba, Anthony. *The History of The American Working Class*. New York: International Publishers Co., INC., 1927. Pg 269

international unions that were connected to the steel industry. Although the meeting was delayed by the hesitant Samuel Gompers, it finally took place on August 1, 1918.[16] The meeting formed the National Committee for Organizing Iron and Steel Workers, represented by one delegate from the twenty four unions concerned with steel. With over two million members, the steel workers were organized to twenty four different unions, working together during the campaign.[17] But when the steel workers were called upon, Samuel Gompers who was the chairman of the committee resigned and disagreed with the union's actions, saying that he would stay faithful to his agreement with Wilson not to organize workers during the war, deserting half a million workers.[18] With the resignation of Gompers, John Fitzpatrick, president of the Chicago Federation of Labor, took over his place.

There were many attempts even by the Amalgamated Association of Iron, Steel, and Tin Workers (AA) to refrain from holding a strike, such as the AA requesting that Judge Gary, chairman of the United States Steel Corporation, to meet and discuss with the representatives of the AA. But he denied this request by saying, "We do not confer, negotiate with, or combat labor unions as such."[19] Then, Gompers wrote a letter to Gary on June 20, 1919, requesting that they negotiate with each other as it was "by American understanding, not by revolutionary methods or the inauguration of a cataclysm," and that he "believe[s] in the effort of employer and employees to sit down around a table."[20] When the unions voted whether to hold a strike, the votes came out to be 98% in favor of holding a strike.[21] With such overwhelming referendum, the committee

---

[16] Ibid.

[17] Brody, David. *Labor in Crisis The Steel Strike of 1919*. Philidelphia: J. B. Lippincott Company, 1965

[18] Bimba, Anthony. *The History of The American Working Class*. New York: International Publishers Co., INC., 1927

[19] Foster, William Z. *The Great Steel Strike and Its Lessons*. New York: B. W. HUEBSCH, INC., 1920.

[20] Ibid.

[21] Brody, David. *Labor in Crisis The Steel Strike of 1919*. Philidelphia: J. B. Lippincott Company, 1965

tried once more to negotiate with Gary. But the result was the same as Gary replied:

> As heretofore publicly stated and repeated, our Corporation and subsidiaries, although they do not combat labor unions as such, decline to discuss business with them. The Corporation and subsidiaries are opposed to the "closed shop." They stand for the "open shop," which permits one to engage in any line of employment whether one does or does not belong to a labor union. This best promotes the welfare of both employees and employers. In view of the well-known attitude as above expressed, the officers of the Corporation respectfully decline to discuss with you, as representatives of a labor union, any matter relating to employees. In doing so no personal discourtesy is intended.[22]

Although receiving a flat refusal from Gary to hold a conference, the committee out of desperation tried one last time to negotiate as they sent a letter to Gary stating, "You question the authority of our committee to represent the majority of your employees. The only way by which we can prove our authority is to put the strike vote into effect and we sincerely hope that you will not force a strike to prove this point."[23] With Gary's reply, the committee then decided to ask President Wilson for his help, regarding the issue between the steel workers and Gary. When Gompers presented the situation, the president promised to induce Gary into having a conference with these men. This allowed for the committee to postpone the strike. But even though a week passed, there was no word from the president or Gary. Foster recites that "with no word from the President. Conditions in the steel industry were frightful. The companies, realizing the importance of striking the first blow, were

---

[22] Gary, Elbert H. Chicago Metro History Education Center. http://www.uic.edu/orgs/cmhec/3_steel.html
[23] Foster, William Z. Chicago Metro History Education Center. http://www.uic.edu/orgs/cmhec/3_steel.html

discharging men by the thousands. The unions could wait no longer. They had to move or be annihilated"[24] The union leaders although afraid from holding a strike, realized that if they did not, they would lose their entire following as thousands were being laid off and were calling for immediate action. But on September 9, 1919, the committee received a telegram from Tumulty,[25] Wilson's secretary, that Wilson did not succeed in arranging a meeting between Judge Gary and the labor union. While the committee asked once more, begging the president to act, Wilson did not act as he was a faithful to the steel trust. The committee, unable to postpone the strike much longer, was forced to declare a strike on September 22, 1919, mobilizing around 365,000 workers.[26]

Even though the strike was declared on September 22, 1919, it faced constant obstacles thrown their way by the employers and even the government. Employers, being challenged by strikes, "used their political and economic leverage to turn public officials, including the police, against the strikers."[27] This is shown as companies hired spies to spread rumors that told the strikes had failed everywhere and gave it as proof of the failure of the steel strike.[28] Then the financial and organizational commitment of the labor unions supporting the Steel Strike, such as AFL and AA, proved to be much more inadequate then expected. Also, employers linked the labor unions and organizations to that of Bolshevism weakening the morale of the workers. The appeals made by the employers connecting the labor unions and organizations to that of Bolshevism not only weakened the morale of workers but also

---

[24] Foster, William Z. *The Great Steel Strike and Its Lessons.* New York: B. W. HUEBSCH, INC., 1920. Pg 84-85
[25] Bimba, Anthony. *The History of The American Working Class.* New York: International Publishers Co., INC., 1927
[26] Brody, David. *Labor in Crisis The Steel Strike of 1919.* Philidelphia: J. B. Lippincott Company, 1965.
[27] Zieger, Robert H., and Gilbert J. Gall. *American Workers, American Unions.* Baltimore: The Johns Hopkins University Press, 2002 pg 40
[28] Rayback, p. 287; Dubofsky and Dulles, p. 220-21; Brody, 1969, p. 254-55.

heightened the fear the public had of communists.[29] They added the labor unions and strikers to their list of the people accused of being socialists or communists. Even the government, who once helped the labor unions acquire their rights and needs, now turned against them. The government, technically not being out of the war as it was still in war with Germany as U.S. did not sign the treaty of Versailles, used its wartime powers against labor unions and their actions. In order to cripple the labor unions and their activities, government agents, "placed union leaders under surveillance, tapped their phones, and threatened them with jail sentences and massive fines."[30] Also Wilson condemned the strikes and although Gompers knew of the government's attitude, he kept it a secret from the AA. This caused the AA to go into strike without knowing that they would have no support.[31] But the main factor that contributed to the downfall was the lack of energy and strength in which the strike fought; as they kept on trying to negotiate when action was necessary.[32] Without support of the government, lack of financial support, and wavering action, it was just a matter of time before the Strike collapsed.

Although the workers and labor unions put in everything they had as a last struggle to win better terms in the factories they worked in, the employers did not give in. By December of 1919 most workers were returning back to their work and jobs. The Committee then finally called off the strike on January 1920.[33] The strike ended in failure on the part of the labor unions and the strikers, as they were unable to achieve any agreement with the employers.

The Great Steel Strike of 1919 was one of the largest strikes ever held in U.S. History. The strike had more than 300,000 members in participation and was held in more than 4 cities. Although it was one of the largest walk-out's in the

---

[29] Brody, David. *Steelworkers in America: The Nonunion Era.* New York: Harper Torchbooks, 1969
[30] Ibid.
[31] Bimba, Anthony. *The History of The American Working Class.* New York: International Publishers Co., INC., 1927
[32] Ibid.
[33]Ibid.

history of the U.S., its result was failure due to many factors. The unwillingness of Gary, the chairman of the U.S. Steel Corporation, to negotiate with the labor unions and workers and the Red Scare during the time contributed majorly to the failure of the strike. While other contributions such as the government support of the corporation and Wilson's support of steel trusts contributed to the downfall of labor unions and their activities.

Bibliography

Primary Sources:

Mitcheel Palmer to the Chamber of Commerce, Moberly, Missouri, Dec. 1, 1919, Department of Labor.

Burgoyne, Arthur G. *Homestead*. Pittsburgh: Harvard College Library, 1893.

Gotlieb, Peter. ""I Witnessed the Steel Strike": Joe Rudiak Remembers the 1919 Strike." History Matters. Available from http://historymatters.gmu.edu/d/106/. Internet; accessed 8 January 2010.

Foster, William Z. *The Great Steel Strike and Its Lessons*. New York: B. W. HUEBSCH, INC., 1920.

Foster, William Z. Chicago Metro History Education Center. http://www.uic.edu/orgs/cmhec/3_steel.html (April 5th, 2010).

Gary, Elbert H. Chicago Metro History Education Center. http://www.uic.edu/orgs/cmhec/3_steel.html (April 5th, 2010).

Wright, Carroll D. JSTOR. http://www.jstor.org/pss/1882283?cookieSet=1. (March 22nd, 2010).

"See Serb Plot in Royal Murders." *New York Times*, 30 June 1914.

Secondary Sources:

Bimba, Anthony. *The History of The American Working Class.* New York: International Publishers Co., INC., 1927.

Brody, David. *Labor in Crisis The Steel Strike of 1919.* Philidelphia: J. B. Lippincott Company, 1965.

Brody, David, *Steelworkers in America: The Nonunion Era.* Harper & Row, 1969.

Dubofsky, Melvyn and Dulles, Foster Rhea. *Labor in America: A History.* 6th ed. Wheeling, IL: Harlan Davidson, Inc., 1999.

Dubofsky, Melvyn. *Hard Work The Making of Labor History.* Chicago: University of Illinois Press, 2000.

Krause, Paul, *The Battle for Homestead, 1880-1892: Politics, Culture, and Steel.* University of Pittsburgh Press, 1992.

Misa, Thomas. A *Nation of Steel The Making of Modern America 1865-1925.* Baltimore and London: The Johns Hopkins University Press, 1995.

Rayback, Joseph G. *A History of American Labor.* Rev. and exp. ed. New York: MacMillan Publishing Co., Inc., 1966.

Robert K. Murray. "Communism and the Great Steel Strike of 1919" *The Mississippi Valley Historical Review,* Vol. 38, No. 3. (Dec., 1951), pp. 445-466. JSTOR.

Standiford, Les. *Meet You In Hell Andrew Carnegie, Henry Clay Frick, and the Bitter Partnership That Transformed America.* New York: Crown Publishers, 2005.

Stohmeyer, John. Crisis *in Bethlehem Big Steel's Struggle to Survive*. New York: Penguin Books, 1986.

Zieger, Robert H., and Gilbert J. Gall. *American Workers, American Unions*. Baltimore: The Johns Hopkins University Press, 2002.

The National Archives. http://www.archives.gov/research/guide-fed-records/groups/002.html (April 2, 2010).

"Alzheimer's Disease: Issues That We Face in Trying to Face the Disease"

Edward Lee
Bergen Academy

Alzheimer's disease is unlike any other disease. Our knowledge about it is limited, and our view of it has changed over the course of the last century. However, as we learn more about the disease and our knowledge advances, we face new obstacles as well. This paper will give a general look at some of the problems that we face in this disease.

Our knowledge of Alzheimer's in the last century

When Alzheimer wrote his paper in 1898, it was not called Alzheimer's disease or AD. Instead, Alzheimer called it "dementia praesenilis". He was the first one who separated it from normal senile dementia. "Praesenilis" implied that the victims of this disease were in their presenium (between the ages of 45 and 65). In 1911, he then published another paper discussing the clinical and morphological changes that a presenile brain with this disease compared to senile brains going through dementia. He went on to explain two major pathological features of the disease; the neurofibrillary tangle and neuritic plaque.

The neurofibrillary tangle occurs when intracellular fibrils thicken and the nerve cell is disrupted. This leaves behind only the "tangled bundle of fibrils" as the only remnant (Katzman and Bick 3).[1]

---

[1] Katzman, Robert, and Katherine Bick. *Alzheimer Disease: The Changing View*. San Diego: Academic Press, 2000. Print.

"Senile or neuritic plaque had first been reported in the brains of old people affected by epilepsy by Blocq and Marinesco working in Paris in 1892 and discussed in detail by Redlich as "miliary sclerosis" in 1892. The term "miliary"... was used to describe lesions or tubercles that had the size and shape of millet seeds" (Katzman and Bick 3).

The plaque seemed to be "an unorganized mass whose appearance is different with different stains..." when it was analyzed by Alzheimer (Katzman and Bick 4). However, upon further analysis by other scientists, this plaque has been shown to have a relationship with amyloids (an insoluble protein that can be deposited in places like the central nervous system) as their reactions to Congo red staining and other characteristics are similar as shown by reports done by Divry (1934) and Scholz (1938); this showed that there are amyloid deposits in Alzheimer plaque. "Scholz found the same characteristics... in the deposits in the cerebral vessel walls and concluded that they were the same as the plaque cores" (Katzman and Bick 4).

Despite all of these new discoveries that were being made, much was still unknown about AD. During the first third of the 20th century, scientists could not distinguish between Alzheimer's and senile dementia. A Canadian-American physician named David Rothschild emerged during the 1930's and 1940's and made important contributions in the relationship between Alzheimer's and senile dementia. He found that there were more lesions present in Alzheimer's and that the "progression of dementia and involvement of language were more severe in the younger cases" (Katzman and Bick 5). But like many other so called "findings" in this obscure disease, later on, Rothschild's conclusion was disproved by R. D. Newton in 1948. R. D. Newton showed that senile dementia and AD were identical. His conclusion was corroborated later on in 1968 by Blessed, Tomlinson, and Roth.

Today, the Alzheimer's Association describes dementia as[2]:

---

2 "2009 Alzheimer's Disease Facts and Figures." Alzheimer's Association, 2009. Web. 26 Aug 2010. <http://www.cdph.ca.gov/programs/alzheimers/Documents/report_alzf actsfigures2009.pdf>.

• *It must include decline in memory and in at least one of the following cognitive abilities:*
1) Ability to generate coherent speech or understand spoken or written language;
2) Ability to recognize or identify objects, assuming intact sensory function;
3) Ability to execute motor activities, assuming intact motor abilities, sensory function and comprehension of the required task; and
4) Ability to think abstractly, make sound judgments and plan and carry out complex tasks.

• *The decline in cognitive abilities must be severe enough to interfere with daily life.*

They also state that Alzheimer's has the following characteristics:

• *Difficulty remembering names and recent events is often an early clinical symptom; apathy and depression are also often early symptoms. Later symptoms include impaired judgment, disorientation, confusion, behavior changes, and trouble speaking, swallowing and walking.*

• *Hallmark abnormalities are deposits of the protein fragment beta-amyloid (plaques) and twisted strands of the protein tau (tangles).*

Obstacles in finding a cure

Advancements in the research of Alzheimer's disease have increased rapidly in the last couple of decades. One may ask, "If research has improved so much and we know so much about the ways to identify AD, why hasn't there been a cure yet?"

Scientists are working on it. Currently, there is one drug called tacrine which has been shown to improve the cognitive effects of AD on a person. There is even hope for more drugs like tacrine that will slow, halt, or even cure the disease completely. However, producing new compounds and drugs is not a simple process. Like all diseases, if people want to find a cure, extensive research must be done. According to the Pharmaceutical Manufacturers of the United States, it costs a pharmaceutical company an *average* of $359 million dollars to get a compound from the laboratory to the pharmacy (qtd. in Cutler and Sramek 87).[3] Although efforts have been made to ameliorate this exorbitant cost that is needed to develop a drug, trying to accomplish that feat with a disease (like Alzheimer's) where little is known will be difficult.

Even as companies and researchers face the challenge of the cost of looking for new drugs or cures, they must also deal with the inevitably lengthy period of time they must devote in order to make a cure into a reality. The Pharmaceutical Manufacturers of the United States reports that a new drug takes an average of 12 years to be developed (qtd. in Cutler and Sramek 87). The reason this process can take so long is because of the thoroughness with which this drug must be tested. Cutler and Sramek say that there are two main steps: preclinical testing and clinical testing. First, scientists must perform preclinical testing, or testing that is done not on humans, but models that may represent a human. This may involve studying the effects of a drug *in vitro* or testing on animals to monitor toxicity and other possible adverse effects the drug may have. However, researchers face another obstacle with animal testing—animals do not get Alzheimer's disease. Instead, researchers must attempt to use old monkeys or rats and compare their cognitive losses to those of people. As science advances however, researchers have been able to genetically engineer a strain of mice that develop amyloid plaques and lose synapses affected by Alzheimer's disease. The transgene that is used is the APP gene (which provides instructions for making a protein called amyloid precursor protein) that is thought to cause early-onset familial Alzheimer's disease. While this seems like a better solution, the only shared characteristics these mice have with Alzheimer's is the overproduction of amyloid proteins resulting in plaques, which may prove not to play a significant role in the disease

---

[3] Cutler, Neal R., and John J. Sramek. *Understanding Alzheimer's Disease*. Jackson MS: University Press of Mississippi, 1996. Print.

compared to others. Despite these drawbacks, they are still useful to test whether a drug can reduce or stop the formation of beta amyloid plaques. Once preclinical testing has been finished, there are also three more phases of clinical testing.

Phase 1: First, after getting sanctioned by the FDA to test the drug on humans, it will be tested in healthy volunteers to determine what dose is appropriate for people. However, when testing people in this stage, researchers face problems unique to Alzheimer's disease. The first issue they face is diagnosis, or whether a patient even has Alzheimer's disease. There are three level so certainty when diagnosing Alzheimer's: possible, probable, and definite. Possible is when the patient has the characteristics of Alzheimer's, but have others as well that are not related to Alzheimer's. Probable is characterized as progressive onset dementia without the possibility of having another brain disorder. Definite diagnosis can only be assigned upon an autopsy and the discovery of neurofibrillary tangles and neuritic plaques. Because of this uncertainty in diagnosing Alzheimer's patients, it is necessary to test the subjects before the experiment begins. Another issue with testing Alzheimer's patients is the difficulty of quantifying the improvement of a patient's condition. Researchers generally test improvement using neuropsychological tests, but the consistency of these tests is questionable because of factors that may affect the results such as mood of the patient, time, and more. Finally, the first stage of clinical testing depends on testing healthy volunteers. This poses a problem because of the fact that not all Alzheimer's patients will be healthy; on the contrary, they will most likely have other complications because of the fact that Alzheimer's manifests itself in the elderly. Elderly people are likely to face complications such as high blood pressure, osteoporosis, and more. Not only do these conditions have the possibility of interfering with the drug for Alzheimer's, they also require regular medication. The medication for the other conditions and the medication for Alzheimer's may have a poor result if a person was to take both at once.

Phase 2: After the first stage, the effectiveness of the drug and possible side effects of long term use are analyzed.

Phase 3: After these two stages, the drug company will submit a drug application to the FDA which can run upwards of 100,000 pages. A committee will read this application and all known data about the particular drug.

Once a drug undergoes this process, it is ready to be released to the public.

Change in care over the years

From 1898 when Alzheimer first wrote his paper until now, much information has been gathered about this disease's pathology. But other aspects of the disease remain unknown; for example, the cause of AD is still a mystery, and consequently, the cure has not been found either. Despite this fact, one cannot simply ignore the treatment of the disease. Although the world does not yet possess the necessary knowledge to cure AD, it is vital that it searches for a way to care for those suffering from AD. People are doing exactly that: searching for ways that Alzheimer's patients can be helped, even if there is no biological cure. To Elaine Brody, Ph.D., the fact that there was no biomedical cure for Alzheimer's did not stop her from discovering ways that she can help Alzheimer's patients.

Elaine Brody started to work for a nursing home called "Home for the Well Aged", meaning that seniors with canes, sicknesses, or mental disabilities were not accepted there. "In the late 1960s there was a big movement nationally to empty mental health hospitals," Elaine Brody says (qtd. in Katzman and Bick 102). As a result of this, old people were pushed out of hospitals and more of them started to look for places like the home Brody worked at. When they were not accepted as patients there, they were found in poor conditions in "boarding homes" that were really "bootleg nursing homes". However, as time went on, Brody started to get the directors to start accepting more people. It started with accepting people with canes, but soon progressed to the acceptance of those with walkers, wheelchairs, and those who are "a little confused", meaning those who may be suffering from dementia.

In 1964, Art Waldman and Powell Lawton were working on designing a building for those with AD. The first step was to hold an Institute on Mentally Impaired Aged. It was "the first international conference focusing on people with Alzheimer's disease" (qtd. in Katzman and Bick 103). The only thing that seemed to be concluded from the meeting however, was that people believed that proper care could not really be administered without a biomedical breakthrough. This fact bothered Brody greatly, and applied and received a grant to research "Individualized Treatment of Mentally Impaired Aged". She helped in the establishment of the Weiss Institute that was dedicated completely to those with AD. Her and Powell Lawton created the ADL (activity of daily living scale), or the Lawton-Brody, as a method to take care of those with AD.

Care giving for the patient

AD is not only the burden of the victim, but also that of the family. It puts strain on the family emotionally, as their own family members forget basic, everyday things, and financially, as the family looks into counseling and treatment. While using the help of a nursing home or professional care may help ameliorate some of the stress of taking care of an AD patient 24/7, many families cannot afford the money necessary for such resources. Not only are the costs of professional care expensive, they are generally much higher for Alzheimer's patients than the costs for regular people of that age group. According to the Alzheimer's Association, health care costs for Alzheimer's patients are several times that of non-Alzheimer's patients. Alzheimer's patients paid an average of $8,000 in hospital payments whereas those in the same age group only paid $3,000. Skilled nursing home costs are even more exorbitant: on average, costs for

Alzheimer's patients were $3,030 compared with $333 for those of other age groups—more than 9 times as much.

However, money is not the only stressor that the caregivers of the patient must worry about. On a study done by Vitaliano, Ph.D., Maiuro, Ph.D., Ochs, Ph.D., and Russo, they attempted to study the stress that aspects of caring for an Alzheimer's patient for spouses.[4] They created a 21 item "Spouse Burden Scale", in which they surveyed spouses on which aspects of care giving they received the most stress. "The items in which the spouses reported the most distress were 'I have little control over my spouse's illness' (82.5 percent reported distress), 'I have little control over my spouse's behavior' (77.8 percent), 'My spouse is constantly asking the same question over and over' (71.4 percent), 'I am upset that I cannot communicate with my spouse' (55.6% percent)..." (277). Vitaliano et al. go on to show how certain patient characteristics can greatly affect the stress that the spouse/caregiver may feel in taking care of the patient. They describe several characteristics that lead to stress, which they categorize as "*maintenance* (e.g., washing eating, mobility) and *higher functioning* (e.g., talking, listening, hobbies) and cognitive deficits such as memory and attention problems..." (277).

AD is one of the most devastating diseases in existence, not only because of its unique pathological and biological effects, but also because of its psychological and sociological effects. In fact, Robert L. Kahn, a psychologist, once called it a "bio-psycho-socio phenomenon" (Kahn, 1975). Kahn stated that although the biological effects are currently untreatable, "the psychological and social are amenable to intervention" (qtd. in Zarit, Orr, and Zarit 2). Zarit, Orr, and Zarit illustrate this statement through the example of Mr. Pine who cares for his wife with AD. When a person with AD misplaces something, they often blame other for it. Because of this tendency, Mr. Pine often got into arguments with his wife. However, a counselor was able to explain to him that AD patients may blame others in order to hide the fact that they could not remember. From that

---

[4] Vitaliano, Peter P., Roland D. Maiuro, Hans Ochs, and Joan Russo. *A Model of Burden in Caregivers of DAT Patients*. Washington, D.C.: U.S. Department of Health and Human Services, 1989. Print.

point on, rather than trying to argue, Pine would acknowledge the fact that she was upset and would ask if he could help in any way. This solution helped prevent further arguing and helped the wife calm down. Cases like Mr. Pine's are common. AD can affect the victim in such a way that it causes tension between family members. This tension often arises from trifling things (in this case, misplacing items), but because of the fact that AD victims frequently try to cover up their memory loss, these matters can grow into fights.

As shown in the case above, caring for an Alzheimer's patient is difficult and requires proper knowledge of how to deal with certain conflicts. Had Mr. Pine not gone to the counselor and received the knowledge required to deal with his wife's spurts of anger, it is likely that the problem would have gone unresolved. Because of the importance of having the knowledge of caring for a patient, many books have been written on the subject, directed towards families who struggle with the burden of having a family member afflicted with the disease. One such book is *Learning to Speak Alzheimer's: A Groundbreaking Approach for Everyone Dealing with the Disease* by Joanne Koenig Coste, former chairperson of the Massachusetts chapter of the Alzheimer's Association.[5] In her book, Coste sets "five tenets of habilitation" that she has developed as she herself had also cared for her husband who had Alzheimer's.

● Tenet #1, she says, is to "make the physical environment work." For Alzheimer's patients, as their memory starts to fade away, their perception of the world will change. This perception is heavily affected by the physical environment, and it is important for the caregiver to facilitate the patient. For example, a patient with Alzheimer's may look at a mirror and not recognize themselves; in this case, the caregiver might remove mirrors from the house or label them with a sign. Some patients may have to go to the bathroom and are unable to find it, and thus are forced to relieve themselves in their pants or even use a closet by accident. In this case, the

---

[5] Coste, Joanne Koenig. *Learning to Speak Alzheimer's: A Groundbreaking Approach for Everyone Dealing with the Disease.* 1st edition. Boston: Houghton Mifflin Company, 2003. Print.

caregiver may make a path that leads to the bathroom in fluorescent tape or put a picture of a bathroom on the door, as pictures are easier to understand than words.

• Tenet #2 is that "communication remains possible." As an Alzheimer's patient's disease goes further, the section of the brain that controls language and ability to communicate will inevitably atrophy as well. Coste says that "often the patient will misuse, bastardize, or alter familiar words altogether" (79), and gives the example of her husband who said "smish" for sandwich. "Smish" eventually came to mean "I'm hungry." It is important to try and understand words (like "smish") that may sound like nonsense, but in actuality have a meaning. The caregiver must also remember that although using words to communicate may be difficult, communications is not limited to words; communication can still go on through emotions such as laughter.

• Tenet #3, Tenet #4, and Tenet #5 are to "focus on remaining skills", "live in the patient's world", and "enrich the patient's life". All of these tenets are focused on protecting the self esteem of the patient, despite some of their eccentricities that may arise as a result of their disease. These tenets try to give the patient the feeling that they are independent by letting them exercise what skills they have left and to reduce possible embarrassment when their memory fails them. Above all, these tenets remind the caregiver to prevent emotional stress for the patient and help them feel independent, despite the effects of the disease.

As Cutler M.D. and Sramek, Pharm.D. say, "Successful caring depends on good communication" (51). While Tenet #2 states that "communication remains possible", one must remember that communication with an Alzheimer's patient cannot be the same as one with a regular person. Therefore, it is important for caregivers to be able to communicate with the patient while reducing the need for them to use their memory. Cutler and Sramek summarize communication techniques with patients as "simplifying what is said, reducing the necessity for patients to use their memory, and helping patients maintain their dignity" (52). In the earliest stages of the disease, it is important to simplify sentences and conversations. While conversing, it is better to sit one on one and to shut off distractions such as TV, music, or other things that may make noise. Before the conversation starts, it is helpful to say an introductory sentence that lets the patient know what the topic will be and to start off with general statements. Sentence structure while talking can be optimized as well in order to help hold a successful conversation. It is best to talk in short simple sentences, avoiding compound sentences and other complex forms. Active voice is superior to passive voice, as it clarifies what is the subject and what is the object. Using active voice is not the only way to help emphasize what the subject of a sentence is: repeating the subject or person's name in every sentence helps as well, rather than replacing the subject with pronouns such as "he" or "it". When asking questions, avoid ones that are open ended. Instead, ask questions that are either "yes" or "no" questions, or ones that give a limited number of choices. Above all, remember to respect the patient. In the later stages of the disease (which Cutler and Sramek classify as the point where the person with Alzheimer's is "disoriented with respect to time and place, fail to recognize… loved ones and are unable to form new memories), it is still important to converse with the patient to prevent their withdrawal. At this point in the disease, factors like tone and face expression become even more vital in the role of communication, as words and sentences are often not understood. While a patient may not be able to understand the exact words that are being said to them, they often still retain the ability to understand the tone and attitude of the speaker. Coste recounted a story in which she went to a home where Alzheimer's patients were conversing and laughing—in different languages. Through laughter, face expressions, and tone alone, they were able to communicate. This is why caregivers must always be aware of their tone, remembering to be reassuring.

Hope

While this paper has focused mainly on the issues we face in Alzheimer's, there is hope. Research in biology has been moving faster than ever. Scientists are discovering new ways with which treatment of Alzheimer's can be improved, and are thinking of new possibilities as well. New diagnostic tools can now be discovered, now that some forms of Alzheimer's have been proven to be a result of a genetic mutation. These genes can now be utilized to help families prepare for the disease early on in its course, and may lead to the discovery of other markers of Alzheimer's as well. Symptomatic treatments in which the symptoms of Alzheimer's are alleviated, but not necessarily the disease, are also being found. A hypothesis called *cholinergic hypothesis* states that raising levels of acetylcholine levels in the brain may compensate for the loss of neurons and cognitive function of the cholinergic system of neurons which produces and uses acetylcholine. Also, preventive treatment to stop Alzheimer's before it emerges has advanced as well. Treatment may take the form of neuroprotective drugs which protect existing neurons for further damage or perhaps the form of tissue transplants.

Although there is no treatment at the moment that can completely cure Alzheimer's, researchers are discovering new treatments that may result in a chain of advancements in this field. With all of these possibilities, it is very possible that one day, there will be a cure for Alzheimer's itself.

Works Cited

Coste, Joanne Koenig. *Learning to Speak Alzheimer's: A Groundbreaking Approach for Everyone Dealing with the Disease*. 1st edition. Boston: Houghton Mifflin Company, 2003. Print.

Cutler, Neal R., and John J. Sramek. *Understanding Alzheimer's Disease*. Jackson MS: University Press of Mississippi, 1996. Print.

Katzman, Robert, and Katherine Bick. *Alzheimer Disease: The Changing View*. San Diego: Academic Press, 2000. Print.

Vitaliano, Peter P., Roland D. Maiuro, Hans Ochs, and Joan Russo. *A Model of Burden in Caregivers of DAT Patients*. Washington, D.C.: U.S. Department of Health and Human Services, 1989. Print.

Zarit, Steven H., Nancy K. Orr, and Judy M. Zarit. *The Hidden Victims of Alzheimer's Disease: Families under Stress*. New York, NY: NYU Press, 1985. Print.

"2009 Alzheimer's Disease Facts and Figures." Alzheimer's Association, 2009. Web. 26 Aug 2010. <http://www.cdph.ca.gov/programs/alzheimers/Documents/report_alzfactsfigures2009.pdf>.

"The Conflict Between Korean-Americans and African-Americans"

Julius Im
Northern Valley Regional High School, Old Tappan

Within society, there are inevitable conflicts that occur even if there are steps taken to avoid conflicts. Such a case of an inevitable conflict is the Korean-American and African-American conflict. In conflicts of society, there are obviously players and several factors that come into the scene that are vital in the creation of the conflict. Without these players and factors, the chances of conflict would heavily decrease. For us to understand the conflict, victimization must be defined and the victims distinguished. Victimization refers to the victims' suffering, including adverse life conditions that follow from the original harm inflicted by the offenders. Victims refer to individuals or a group of individuals who suffer harm (psychological, social, cultural, economic, political) inflicted by others, the offenders; victims are not responsible for the harm. The players involved must also be identified; obviously, Korean-Americans and African-Americans are two of the key players involved. However, there is a third major player, the white society, which branches out into a number of different factors that contribute to the conflict. The history of each player must be observed as well, in order to better understand the causes of the conflict.

The conflict between African-Americans and Korean-Americans could be said to have started before the 1990's, but was simply exploited and labeled as a "conflict" after 1992. Before 1992, there were cases involving discontent between Korean store owners and African-American customers. Korean store owners were claimed to be "rude" by the African-American customers because they were ignored and neglected even as customers. The Korean store owners on the other hand, claimed the African-American customers to be just as rude because of their harsh language, swearing, and inadequate behavior. Even something as small as this scenario contributes to the conflict between Koreans and African-Americans. Misconceptions also play a role; African-American residents of inner-city regions, such as in Los Angeles and New York City, believed that Koreans were attempting to overrun the African-American residential area with Korean businesses so that African-American businesses could no longer flourish. The African-American populace of these areas believed that Koreans were simply trying to gain economic power and eventually overtake the African-American residents for the benefit of the Koreans, and this is where history is a vital aspect to observe from in order to clarify these misconceptions.

By the 1930's, the perimeters of African American settlements were well established in most cities. The Great Depression caused a great number of African Americans out of the rural South, almost four hundred thousand migrants from the period of 1930-1940. The African-American migrants from the south to the cities of the north continued on, and as this migration continued, segregation was a constant. The migrants that flowed into the cities were inevitably segregated from the white society and set apart as a different black society. This segregation evidently explains the reason there are densely populated African-American districts even today. The discrimination against African-Americans did not end with segregation, but expanded towards occupational discrimination. These two factors, segregation and occupational discrimination undeniably corroborated the environment that African-Americans were to live in until the present. The racial discrimination was simply worsened by the fact that the U.S. government began deindustrialization of the inner city regions and shifted the economy from manufacturing to service-oriented industries. Through deindustrialization of these inner cities, several jobs were eliminated, thus creating a high rate of unemployment which inevitably affected the majority of young male workers. Because of the high rate of unemployment, marriage is delayed on the basis of financial problems which results in out-of-wedlock births and single parent, female-headed households. This unemployment further create an opportunity for the underground society to take over; drug trafficking, prostitution, and gambling all take over as a means to mediate for the jobs that disappeared along with deindustrialization. With this degradation of African-American living in addition to an arduous past, the dignity of the African-Americans was the only thing left for them, which could explain why African-American customers are infuriated when they are ignored by Korean businessmen.

With underground society careers overrunning the inner cities filled with African-Americans, the white society leaves these areas because businesses in such areas are not appealing to the white society. This is when the Korean immigrants from South Korea come in to play their role, and occupy the jobs that the white society has discarded as unappealing. And the issue with the Koreans is that they must indubitably accept the jobs that the white society does not desire. Korean immigrants that moved to the United States were without doubt, educated and experienced in the occupational world. However, because the U.S. government did not recognize the merits and educational achievements these Koreans had achieved at Korean universities and schools, they were essentially "starting from scratch". The Koreans had three options regarding their occupations: 1. Occupations with short supply of workers 2. Occupations avoided or disdained by native-born whites 3. Low wage and low skill occupations. Koreans, having experience in the occupational world, preferred not to work in low wage jobs, which is the reason why the majority of the immigrants from Korea began their own businesses, such as fruit vendors, dry cleaners, and restaurants. Evidently, Koreans were not attempting to push African-Americans out of their residents, but simply needed a feeding ground which would not take a toll upon them economically.

Indeed, Koreans were acting as the "middle-man minority" rather than as a force attempting to sabotage the African-American residents. The middle-man minority essentially describes the situation in which foreign/ethnic entrepreneurship arrives in a geographic location where it becomes a recognizable minority and is rejected from entering the primary labor market (in this case the Koreans). These entrepreneurs are inevitably forced to engage in basic types of entrepreneurial activities and in the case of the Koreans, small businesses such as street vendors, dry-cleaners, and restaurants. The Koreans filled the low-income areas, which explains the reason why a large majority of Korean service and retail businesses are located in nonwhite, low-income areas. These areas are areas that native-born whites ignore and think of as undesirable, which leaves only the immigrants to occupy them. This is essentially how Koreans are considered as the middleman minority. The white society and African-American society are both separated and the Koreans come in between acting not necessarily as mainstream society but as mediators of the white society and African-American society.

After observing the African-Americans' situation, it is essential to acknowledge the Koreans' culture and aspect. African-American customers who claimed Korean store-owners were supposedly "rude" to them did not take into consideration the environment in which Koreans were raised and nurtured in. Within Korean society, respect and courtesy are of high expectations, which means proper etiquette in public is absolutely necessary. So when African-American customers swear and use harsh languages in places such as Korean fruit stores or dry cleaners, they tend to be ignored because they are not showing respect in Korean standards. By Korean standards, an individual will be ignored if he or she is not deserving of respect and in the case of the African-American customers, in the eyes of Koreans, they were not deserving of respect because of their foul language and inappropriate conduct within their businesses. However, African-American customers misunderstood this Korean standard because within American society, customers deserve unchallenged respect and service no matter the circumstance. And because of these two conflicting ideologies, conflict was further provoked and tensions grew higher. In another instance, African-American customers claimed that Korean store owners were "rude" in the sense that they did not smile. This is an interesting aspect because it also coincides with Korean culture. In America, smiling is a friendly gesture whether it is to a friend or to a stranger and knows no bounds. Despite this friendly gesture, Korea views it in a completely different manner. In the Korean context, if a woman smiles at a man she does not know, it is assumed that she is a prostitute. Clearly, there is a distinction between two cultures which are obscured by each other, resulting in an unpleasant relationship between two minority factions.

It is important however, to observe the relationship between Koreans and the white society as well as African-Americans and the white society. The Koreans within the white society primarily do not receive help from the white society. When the Koreans came from South Korea, they were required to create their businesses themselves; they gained no government help, no special funds, and no loans. The Koreans built everything on their own and supported the businesses by themselves. Clearly, the relationship between Koreans and the white society is already evidently weak and unappealing. To worsen the status of the relationship, the Koreans contributed financially toward political figures in order to ensure that they had some form of political power and security in times of need. However, despite the contributions the Koreans made, no white political figure made efforts to save his or her Korean "friends" during instances such as the LA Riots. Instead, the white society averted the destruction of white businesses and property by redirecting the riot towards Koreatown. It is more than clear that the white society was unwilling to protect a minority such as the Koreans.

The relationship between African-Americans and the white society is even worse than that of the relationship between the Koreans. Firstly, the white society has abused the African-American population for decades without end and when African-Americans actually received civil rights, they were simply segregated from the white society. The white society absolutely despised the African-American population that it set them apart from it and took away jobs from them, leaving them to deteriorate economically, socially, and politically. The white society primarily provoked and caused uprisings of African-

Americans such as in the LA riots. The LA riot was first provoked when Latasha Harlins, a 15-year old African-American female was shot and killed by a Korean woman named Soon Da Ju, who was simply given a probation and a $500 fine. As one individual put it, "You get sent to jail for killing a dog, you get a probation for killing a black person." The judge adjudicating the case of Latasha Harlin was white, and this caused agitation between African-Americans and whites. To worsen the already tense situation, in the case of Rodney King, in which an African-American male was beat by several police officers even after he submitted, the officers who had committed police brutality were acquitted. It is evident that these officers should have received a harsh punishment, but looking at the court case, it is also clear that racial discrimination plays a key factor. Because the white society had political dominance over the African-Americans, they utilized it in a manner that would benefit the white society rather than justify the African-Americans. It is undeniably evident that the relationship between African-Americans and the white society and Koreans and the white society are both less than adequate.

The media is a large part of the Korean and African-American conflict as well. The media tends to exaggerate as it does in everything. For instance in the LA riot, the media portrayed Koreans as gun-slinging vigilantes when Koreans simply did not have the political power to send out a message that they were simply protecting their businesses. The media rejected any message of the Koreans and claimed that there was a "black-Korean-American conflict" occurring when the Koreans were simply in the "wrong place at the wrong time". The primary target of the African-Americans was the white businesses in areas such as Beverly Hills, but when the LAPD diverted the riot, it coincidentally flowed into Koreatown, a convenient route that the riot took.

Even before Korean immigrants moved to the United States, the media heavily influenced the mindset of Koreans. During the intervention of the United States for Korea during World War II and during the Korean War, the American media was brought along with the troops dispatched in Korea. During those years that the United States troops were in Korea, they displayed American media, films, and television to the Koreans. In these films and television that the American media showcased, African-Americans were inevitably discriminated and labeled as stereotypically lazy, poor, thieves, thugs, immoral, and drug abusers. Clearly, because of white media, the Koreans had a pre-determined mindset of what African-Americans were, and thus attained a racist mindset (at least towards African-Americans) even before they set foot on America. It is obvious that the white media does not portray the African-Americans' point of view and their history. The white media does not focus upon the fact that the white society essentially placed African-Americans into a state of depredation and in this way, it is a corrupt influence upon Korean society. Because of the white media, Koreans conjured a mindset that believed African-Americans were uneducated and basically inhuman. The Koreans failed to understand the history of the African-Americans; the fact that African-Americans were abused, furthermore segregated, and eventually discriminated occupationally. The white media evidently exploits both sides in a negative manner. The African-Americans are clearly exploited in that they are portrayed as a group of degenerate people who are uneducated and lazy, which ultimately influences the opinions of the Korean minority. The Korean minority, during the LA riot, is exploited just as equally because they are portrayed as "gun-slinging vigilantes" when in actuality they are simply acting to defend their hard-earned businesses. The white media is evidently a crippling factor to both minorities and it is seemingly similar to a player in chess; the white media symbolizes the player moving the chess pieces, and the African-American and Korean minorities act as pawns, which the player pits against each other.

Having observed all the major relationships: white society to African-Americans, white society to Koreans, role of media, and the history of the white society between the two minorities, it is essential to understand that a single occurrence does not cause the breakout of a conflict. For instance, in New York City, there were several cases of Korean business owners acting "rude" towards African-American customers. This issue of disrespect may have potentially caused the boycott of Korean businesses in New York City, but how the conflict is created at the collective level and further developed is completely different from the nature and the cause of the conflict.

The conflict commences when one or more players in the conflict take collective action. As in the case of New York City, several African-American customers claimed they were treated with disrespect in the Korean businesses. From this, they emphasized the issue of "disrespect" and the legitimacy of a boycott was stressed. Economic empowerment was a key goal of the boycott: By African-Americans boycotting Korean stores, these Koreans could be run out of business since these businesses were located in heavily black concentrated neighborhoods. Personal political empowerment acted as an incentive for the people leading the boycott and the movements/marches. The African-Americans regarded non-blacks as "outsiders" (Koreans)-who simply exploited blacks and did not represent black interests. Clearly, the cause of the conflict between African-Americans and Koreans is entirely separate from the creation of the conflict at a collective level. The African-American community declared a boycott and attempted to "Africanize" the black community; they attempted to ethnicize the community of black people no matter where they were from. The simple end of "Africanizing" was essentially to gain human power—utilize human resources to conjure political power in order to attain economic power. They labeled all blacks as African-Americans in order to effectively boycott Korean stores; achieve a political unity in order to boost their political power. The African-Americans of New York City disregarded the ethnicity of all blacks and essentially united them under one category.

In the midst of collective action, it is imperative to understand and comprehend the factors underlying the motives behind collective action. Within the African-American community of New York City, there were personal political incentives; the African-American leaders were essentially locked in a power struggle against one another. In order to attain power, these leaders attempted to mobilize the boycotts and marches demonstrating against Korean businesses in order to create an image which was that of a leader. The issue with the African-American minority and the Korean minority is that, the African-

American interpersonal dispute was exacerbated and exaggerated in a manner that eventually spawned an intergroup conflict. However, apart from this small inter-minority dispute, there is a larger one, which is again, of the African-American minority and the dominant white society. The African-Americans, in an effort to conjure political power against the dominant white society, attempted to take action by driving out Korean businesses in order to replace them with African-American businesses. By doing so, African-Americans of the area could then corroborate economic power which would then help impact political status. The African-American population is more intent on gaining political power and challenging the dominant white society rather than taking away power from Koreans because they dislike Koreans. However, it is evident that the African-Americans utilized the Koreans conveniently as a means of scapegoating, in order to obtain the political and economic power to challenge the dominant white society. Again, it is clear that the Koreans are simply "in the wrong place, at the wrong time" and are stuck in the middle between a larger conflict between the dominant white society and the minority African-Americans.

However, that is not to say that Koreans did not provoke anti-Korean sentiments in the African-Americans; they did in part arrive in America with anti-black prejudices. As stated earlier, Koreans had been heavily influenced by American media since World War II with American intervention to liberate Korea from Japanese rule and again in the Korean War to avert communist influence. This American media that arrived in Korea during the 20th century ultimately composed in the Koreans, a predetermined mindset about African-Americans. So, when Koreans arrived in America and began their businesses, some individuals would mark African-Americans with negative connotations. In New York City, several individuals stated similar comments such as, "Blacks cannot own and manage this kind of business. They are lazy. They are too ignorant. They don't have business skills and stamina." Additionally, prejudiced comments existed, such as "for the low-class blacks, especially, they are so much accustomed to enjoying their lives without working. No job is not a stigma to them any more. I firmly believe that if all Korean merchants pack and leave this area, and blacks take over, this block will become a slum again." It is without doubt that many of these Korean business owners are slightly if not extremely prejudiced against African-Americans and that they have been influenced by American media stereotypes of African-Americans. What endorses the idea that the Koreans were prejudiced is the fact that several Koreans in the area used derogatory terms in order to speak about African-Americans, such as "camdungi" (Korean for "nigger") in place of the formal term of "heuk in" (Korean for "black person"). In New York City, a campaign to educate Korean merchants on how to prevent and avoid problems with black customers was taken by the *Korean Times New York*, which issued an article with the title, "Ten Essentials for the Prevention of Black-Korean Conflict" (September 28, 1991). The first rule of this list required the abolishment of the use of the word "camdungi", and the last of the rules mentioned is discontinuance of the idea that "black=ignorant". Just the mere fact that a campaign was taken clarifies the fact that Koreans have been heavily influenced by racism and prejudice that was displayed in American media. And because of the influence by American media, Koreans simply provoked the African-American community to utilize them as a scapegoat.

It is not simply the Koreans' anti-black sentiments, however, but that both Koreans and African-Americans are conscious of their political status. The Koreans and African-Americans are both minority groups when compared to the dominant white society, and they are both well aware of their situation. And this very situation, the minority status, is what places both groups into a state of caution. Because they are both minority groups, each wants to establish dominance over the other because although both groups cannot take on the dominant society, they can at the very least try to control the other group because it is similar in strength. The Koreans were economically strong but politically weak, while vice versa, the African-Americans were politically strong but economically weak. And because of the consciousness between one another's statuses, they try to assert some aggression and instill some form of sternness within the other. With that said, an example of this form of aggression would be a Korean storeowner displaying a stern manner when a customer approaches or constantly watching his customers. There are three types of consciousness between these groups, which are racial, ethnic, and minority consciousness. For African-Americans, racial consciousness is a critical issue because of the history of racial discrimination they have suffered, and therefore, many black customers may have interpreted certain behaviors by Korean store owners as offensive, racist, and believe that they are being treated differently because they are black. Ethnic consciousness is also prevalent, especially in Haitian Americans. They have been claimed to have connections to AIDS, which ultimately strained ethnic resentment and caused a rally against the prejudice on April 20, 1990. Finally, Koreans inevitably suffer the minority consciousness because they are inclined to think that they are mistreated by the neighborhood blacks because they have no significant power.

Consciousness does play a role in straining social relations, however, within the context of the Korean and African-American conflict, New York City illustrates that structural contradictions in Korean businesses account for a great deal of resentment between African-Americans and Koreans. A number of Korean stores, or the majority of Korean stores are somewhere between a small grocery shop and a supermarket such as Shoprite. These stores are mid-sized stores, somewhere around 1,800 to 2,000 square feet with around 7 to 10 employees. The size of the store restricts storeowners from monitoring and controlling their customers. To monitor the customers, the storeowners would need some form of surveillance, but even surveillance would be too costly for the middle class storeowners to afford. Therefore, the only convenient solution to the problem of monitoring is simply by watching. The problem with watching the customers is that it emits an unfriendly atmosphere, almost as if the storeowner is regarding the customer as a thief rather than a valued customer; this is part of where negative sentiment begins. These convenience stores most probably have low prices, because of the competition that exists among other Korean storeowners, and therefore in these stores exist several customers. When there are several customers, the storeowner or cashier does not have the time to properly thank the customer or display utmost respect, and therefore may dissatisfy the customer.

The solution to the conflict between the two minority factions, African-Americans and Koreans, is not simple, but with better understanding of the conflict and the history of the two communities, interethnic harmony can be achieved. And it is in this spirit, I have conducted this study.

"Thomas Edison"

Kevin Lee
Ridgewood High School

Thomas Alva Edison, the most eminent and prolific American inventor was born to a middle class family in Feb. 11, 1847, in Milan, Ohio, the second largest wheat shipping center in the world. He was the last of seven children, and didn't learn to speak until four. At age seven, his family moved to Port Huron, Michigan, a frontier town with opportunities in real estate speculations and lumbering and a city which surpassed the commercial superiority of Milan[1]. He attended a school with 38 other children of various ages.

Young Alva (called "Al" when young) was always curious and would ask an adult how things worked. Only after 3 months, his short tempered teacher lost his patience with Alva's unrelenting questions and ostensibly narcissistic behavior. The teacher noted that Alva's forehead was very broad and that his head was larger than average, so he did not make it a secret that he thought Alva's brain was scrambled[2]. Alva's mother noticed the situation and quickly took him out of school to home-school him, since she was a formal school teacher herself. Unlike the school teacher, she was certain that Alva's abnormal demeanor was a sign of extreme intelligence. His mother, Nancy Edison,

---

1 Gerald Beals, "The Biography of Thomas Edison." Thomas Edison.com 1999, 29 August 2010.
<http://www.thomasedison.com/biography.html>.
2 Gerald Beals, "The Biography of Thomas Edison." Thomas Edison.com 1999, 29 August 2010.
<http://www.thomasedison.com/biography.html>.

could focus on Thomas, since three of her seven children were dead, and the other three were much older.

At home, his mother taught him the Bible, and his father Samuel Edison made him read classical books. Soon, Thomas developed an interest in history and English literature. He considered being an actor, but he soon gave up the idea due to his high pitched voice and his shyness before an audience. After reading many books in the library, Thomas showed interests in the sciences, however he learned too much that even his parents couldn't comprehend what he was asking. He was only 11 at that time. His parents hired a tutor to help their son understand things. Thomas did have a love for science, but he hated how the textbooks such as Newton's *Principia* were written in such "high tone" language that was confusing to the average person[3]. His father also encouraged him to study politics, but Thomas was not interested. However, he showed an entrepreneurial interest. At twelve he quit his home studies as he became interested in making money, and he became a newsboy on a train from Port Huron to Detroit. While on the train, he saw marketing opportunities with comestibles. He bought goods cheaply in the big city, and opened a fresh produce stand and newsstand in Port Huron. Of course, loading the train with baskets of vegetables was not a very acceptable act, but Thomas knew how to make the trainmen cooperate by giving fresh goods for a cheap price[4]. He also hired two other boys to help him with his business.

At age fifteen, he expanded his newspaper business, using a second hand galley-proof press. Luckily for him, a British passenger bought his entire run of "weekly Herald" and Edison soon heard that he was mentioned in the *London Times* as being the first person to print newspapers on a train[5]. Since he was also interested in science, he set up a chemistry laboratory in

---

3 Gerald Beals, "The Biography of Thomas Edison." Thomas Edison.com 1999, 29 August 2010.
<http://www.thomasedison.com/biography.html>.
[4] Randall Stross, *The Wizard of Menlo Park*.(United States of America: Crown Publishers 2007). 4
[5] Randall Stross, *The Wizard of Menlo Park*.(United States of America: Crown Publishers 2007). 4

the baggage car. However, when a bottle of phosphorus fell and caught on fire, Thomas' lab and newspaper printing press was ejected from the train. He also got a blow to the head from the angry conductor, which might have worsened his hearing. One day, Edison was lucky enough to see the station agent James Mackenzie's young son on the train track, about to get rolled over. The child's mother fainted, but Edison was just quick enough to save the child. Mr. Mackenzie was grateful and taught Edison how to use the Morse code and the telegraph as his reward.

Soon, Thomas had mastered the art, and acquired a career as a replacement for the thousands of "Brass Pounders" (telegraph operators) who had gone to the civil war. He now had a chance to improve his speed and efficiency in sending and receiving code. He also did some experiments of his own, and at age sixteen, he made his first authentic invention, the automatic repeater. This device transmitted signals between unmanned stations, and made it easy for anyone to translate code[6]. However, he never patented this initial version. When he was sixteen, he was working for the Grand Truck Railroad, and he was to work for the night shift at Stratford Junction, Ontario. One night, he was told to send a message to hold a freight train that would arrive soon on one side, since another train just left from the opposite side on the single track. When Edison ran out to find the signalman, the freight train he was supposed to stop flew past. There was only one chance to stop the train, and it was to get to where the daytime operator was so he could send a signal to avoid collision. However, he fell in a culvert and was knocked out. The collision was avoided since the train operators saw each other in time and stopped. The next day, he and his immediate supervisor were called to the main office in Toronto, Canada. The main superintendent was curious why Edison, only 16 had a job with so much responsibility, and threatened to put him in jail for criminal negligence. However, Edison was lucky. Suddenly three English visitors appeared and made a distraction. In that time, Edison fled and took the train to the United States.

---

[6] Gerald Beals, "The Biography of Thomas Edison." Thomas Edison.com 1999, 29 August 2010.
<http://www.thomasedison.com/biography.html>.

While in the US, he still worked as a telegraph operator for the next five years in areas such as Adrian, Michigan, Fort Wayne, Indianapolis, Cincinnati, Memphis, and Louisville. He worked as a part of the "tramp operators" Fraternity. In this club, technical skill operating the apparatus and creativity in practical jokes were prized, and Edison was highly regarded by other members on both things[7]. He was a great receiver, writing very fast. Also, he was creative in inventing for the cause of fun. For example, he would use batteries used for the telegraph machines to use them for pranks involving electric shocks.

For his experiments with the telegraph, he would often buy equipments with his own wages. So, one day he returned home deprived of money. However, his parents were in an even worse predicament. His mother seemed to be insane, and his father quit his job; the bank was about to foreclose on their home. Following his friend Billy Adams' suggestion, he moved to Boston to get a job in the prestigious Western Union Company. He had been given some free rail tickets, and was convinced to move since Boston was considered the center of science, education, and culture. And when he arrived in Boston in 1868 to work as a night shift operator, he was hungry and penniless. He was, "The worst looking specimen of humanity I ever saw," described by an operator who witnessed him[8]. His clothing were didn't fit him. However poor he was, he easily passed the exam and was hired. He was allowed to tinker during his free time, and he soon sought investors who would give him money in exchange for half interest in resulting patents. He soon started working on inventing things such as improved telegraph transmitters, fire alarm using telegraph, a stock price printer, and an electric vote recorder. The first invention that worked was the vote recorder. However, the Congress disliked it because it recorded votes too fast. They liked having some time in manual counts so each member could think more about their votes. After the rejection, Edison vowed to only invent things that would be of commercial needs.

---

[7] Randall Stross, *The Wizard of Menlo Park*.(United States of America: Crown Publishers 2007). 5

[8] Randall Stross, *The Wizard of Menlo Park*.(United States of America: Crown Publishers 2007). 7

After a year at the Western Union, in 1869 he quit his job and became a full time inventor. He became well respected and well liked, and also well trusted. He didn't have the education and financial support unlike other inventors, but he didn't mind. Also, his deafness didn't bother him. In fact, he said that the silence gave him time to think out his problems and later in life said that he was lucky to have not listened to "all the foolish conversation and other meaningless sounds that normal people hear."[9] Since he thought most sounds people heard were meaningless, he also avoided drinking which would interfere with his learning and inventing.

At first, his inventing business was only supported by some willing friends, and his modest goal was to achieve autonomy. However, he would later patent an astonishing 1093 inventions, by himself and jointly. He moved around from Boston to New York, and then to Newark working in businesses such as "Newark Telegraph Works," "News Reporting Telegraph Company" with a partner. Sometimes, Edison's partner and his name appeared on the name of their company "Pope, Edison & Company," and as time went by, his name appeared first, signifying his importance in their company, such as the "Edison and Unger," and "Edison and Murray."[10]

Some days, their company did well, and other times not too well. He also tried to be an entrepreneur, and after 3 years with William Unger, in 1872, his half share of the company was worth about $11,438[11]. He also worked with Unger in the News Reporting Telegraph Company. The idea of this company, to enable people to buy news from a private telegraph line and printer that delivered news hours before it was published was about a century ahead of its time. However, some people such as businessmen could convert the news into their financial gain before others could. When Edison and his partner opened the company, one of their hired employees was a sixteen year old

---

[9] Randall Stross, *The Wizard of Menlo Park*.(United States of America: Crown Publishers 2007). 9

[10] Randall Stross, *The Wizard of Menlo Park*.(United States of America: Crown Publishers 2007). 13-14

[11] Randall Stross, *The Wizard of Menlo Park*.(United States of America: Crown Publishers 2007). 14

Mary Stillwell. Edison was fond of her and married her; at the time of marriage he was twenty-four. By this time, Edison was prosperous enough to buy a home in Newark with servants and $2000 worth of furnishings. According to one source, Mary Edison did not like his husband as the inventor genius and tried to make him into a well dressed sociable person. Also, their firstborn girl Marion, born in 1873, remembered her several birthday parties given by her mother that her father never attended, which tells that Mrs. Edison failed to convert Mr. Edison[12].

Edison was also wealthy through the selling of his inventions and opened a laboratory in Newark. He also gave money to her parents and helped financially with his father's and brother's business in Port Huron. He owned five businesses in Newark, but they were dependent, however, in client firms in the telegraph business, who were also dependent on the Wall Street Firms. So, like most businesses, when the Panic of 1873 hit, he too was hit hard and sold his house to move to an apartment. However, he still worked in his laboratory. One thing he tried was the duplex telegraphy. However, he was quite unfortunate. A supervisor where he worked fired him for being an idiot in terms of the supervisor's thoughts since there seemed to be no way that a wire could be worked both ways at the same time. Also, he was too late and someone else had already patented the idea. Edison just worked harder and developed the quadruplex transmitter, using complex electromechanical devices, which solidified his reputation in the telegraphy field, and a company paid $40,000 for his invention[13].

At age 29, he worked with carbon transmitters, which ultimately made Alexander Graham Bell's amazing telephone. Edison was disappointed that Bell had beaten him in the invention, and went on to invent the commercially practical incandescent electric light bulb.

---

[12]Randall Stross, *The Wizard of Menlo Park*.(United States of America: Crown Publishers 2007). 16

[13] Gerald Beals, "The Biography of Thomas Edison." Thomas Edison.com 1999, 29 August 2010. <http://www.thomasedison.com/biography.html>.

Many people equate Edison with inventing the light bulb, but it is a little exaggerated. Edison was a great man because of how he manipulated his and other's cleverness.[14] The light bulb was invented decades before, and there were two types, the fluorescent and incandescent light bulb. In 1808, Humphrey Davey of England produced the light bulb and demonstrated how it worked in front of the Royal Society. It worked by electric flows leaping across a gap, or by heating an element until it glowed white[15]. There were tests of these light bulbs, but most were not commercial and some were too bright. Edison worked for a long time to fix these problems, and finally came up with his masterpiece. He was mastering his invention, and because of it, he knew that stock prices all over the country depended on whether his discovery was true or not. His friend wrote in a letter that the British equivalent of $1.36 billion was "trembling in its balance,"[16] and that British scientists were trying to find if his discovery was true. Also, his rival William Sawyer claimed that Edison infringed some of his inventions and that the light bulb won't last ten minutes. He also claimed that Edison was only trying to raise money in the capital market. On the first day of the demonstration in Menlo Park, December 26th 1879, his friends were invited to see the light. The next day, Newspaper agencies, and numerous spectators had arrived to watch his light bulb. The demonstration started with few streetlamps being lighted, then as more unexpected spectators gathered around to see the light, Edison lighted more lamps. By New Year's Eve, there were extra trains to Menlo Park, and the laboratory added more stunts, such as putting a light bulb completely under water. Edison claimed that the light bulb would last for up to thirty years, and he himself was in his work clothes answering questions. *The New York Herald* noted Edison as "a simple young man attired in the homeliest manner, using for his

---

[14] Harold Evans, *They Made America*. (United States of America: Little, Brown and company, 2004) 152

[15] Randall Stross, *The Wizard of Menlo Park*.(United States of America: Crown Publishers 2007). 76

[16] Randall Stross, *The Wizard of Menlo Park*.(United States of America: Crown Publishers 2007). 83

explanation not high sounding technical terms, but the plainest and simplest language."[17]

By New Year's Day, the number of the crowd was unmanageable. Some spectators threatened to take down Edison's laboratory, and the lab assistants also caught an electrician hired by the Baltimore Gas Company trying to short circuit some of Edison's light bulbs, and on January 2nd, he closed his lab from the public.[18] Edison also received an offer from J.P. Morgan and Edison's workers installed his Italianate Mansion with the electric light on June 8th 1882. The workers finished the installment of 385 lights by fall.[19].

Thomas Edison was a celebrity; in fact, one of the first ones that were not a politician or military figure. He was famous for his inventions in electricity, batteries, mining, and telegraphs, but the most important invention that made him the celebrity with his fame exceeding any others was the phonograph. He was quoted saying "Of all my inventions, I liked the phonograph best"[20]. Edison had the basic patents, and later inventors such as Emile Berliner would perfect it since Edison's was hard to duplicate [21] . Of course there were other more important inventions that affected the U.S economy, but the phonograph, with the power to play sounds, instantly seized the imagination of people who heard about it, as Edison had especially liked it. Other inventions by other inventors such as the steamboat by Robert Fulton, and the reaper by Cyrus McCormick, or Eli Whitney's cotton gin would not have the same impact on people's mind. The phonograph was invented after 1877, when

---

[17] Randall Stross, *The Wizard of Menlo Park*.(United States of America: Crown Publishers 2007). 103-104

[18] Randall Stross, *The Wizard of Menlo Park*.(United States of America: Crown Publishers 2007). 105

[19] Jill Jonnes, *Empires of Light:Edison, Tesla, Westinghouse, and the Race to Electrify the World*.(United States of America: Random House, 2003). 6

[20] Gerald Beals, "Thomas Edison Quotes." Thomas Edison.com 1999, 29 August 2010. <http://www.thomasedison.com/biography.html>.

[21] David J. Cole, Eve Browning, and Fred E.H. Schroeder. *Encyclopedia of Modern Everyday Inventions*. (United States of America: Greenwood Press, 2003.) 194

Edison had the idea to record messages in Bell's telephone. It was completed and put on the market by 1878. It fascinated people, but it was not very successful. However, the later versions of it such as the musical phonograph were extremely successful, and by 1907, he had sold 20 million records.[22]

By the 1920's Edison was also internationally known; however, he had very few close friendships. Even at an old age, he kept working until his health began to fail. He still worked, but mostly at home, until his 1093rd patent at age 83. Edison passed away at 9 P.M Oct 18th 1931, when he was 84. His death marked an end in an era of progress of civilization, and countless individuals mourned his death. Many realized that, though Edison was imperfect, he was essentially good, proud that he is "proud of the fact that I never invented weapons to kill...,"[23] and that he did more than anyone for the betterment of mankind.

---

[22] Harold Evans, *They Made America*. (United States of America: Little, Brown and company, 2004) 156

[23] Gerald Beals, "Thomas Edison Quotes." Thomas Edison.com 1999, 29 August 2010. <http://www.thomasedison.com/biography.html>.

Bibliography

Cole, David J., Eve Browning, and Fred E.H. Schroeder. *Encyclopedia of Modern Everyday Inventions*. United States of America: Greenwood Press, 2003.

Evans, Harold. They Made America. United States of America: Little, Brown and company, 2004.

Gerald Beals, "The Biography of Thomas Edison." Thomas Edison.com 1999, 29 August 2010. <http://www.thomasedison.com/biography.html>.

Jonnes, Jill. *Empires of Light:Edison, Tesla, Westinghouse, and the Race to Electrify the World*. United States of America: Random House, 2003.

Stross, Randall. *The Wizard of Menlo Park*. United States of America: Crown Publishers, 2007.

"Gabrielle Coco Chanel"

Julia Jeon
The Academy of Holy Angels

Gabrielle Coco Chanel, the only person in the field of fashion to be named on *Time 100: The Most Important People of the Century*, was a very independent woman who worked from the bottom of the fashion field to be the starter of grand fashion brand, Chanel. Her every collection and new designs received the massive of attention over the world and her liberal view of woman's fashion especially for their freedom and simplicity brought great changes to fashion over the century and to today's fashion. Modernist philosophy, menswear-inspired fashions, and pursuit of expensive simplicity made her an important figure in 20th-century fashion. A safari jacket and skirt in jersey, fur-trimmed capes and pocketed coats, all had an easy air of nonchalance. Indeed, America not only promoted her fashions, it even inspired her styles. A satin cowboy dress fringed in silk won a large feature in *Vogue* (Wallach 28). "For hundred years, Coco Chanel has been synonymous with every piece of clothing we consider stylish" (Karbo 3). However, Gabrielle Chanel's outstanding talent was not discovered from the beginning.

Gabrielle Coco Chanel was born on 19 August 1883 in Saumur in France. She was one of six children of Albert Chanel, a market stallholder, and Jeanne Devolle, a laundry woman. Even though Chanel had many siblings, she preferred to play alone with her dolls. In her early year, she followed her dad, Albert Chanel, to the market. In the market, Gabrielle Chanel indirectly experienced the wealthy life through wealthy customers in the markets, and Gabrielle Chanel played the role of wealthy woman with her dolls. From this year, Gabrielle

Chanel dreamed to be wealthy like them one day. From her early years, Gabrielle Chanel was independent and ambitious. Therefore, even though she was from a poor family, she acted with pride and elegance as she grew up with her family. However, in 1895, Gabrielle Chanel's mom, Jeanne Devolle, died from tuberculosis. Then, as soon as Jeanne Devolle died, Gabrielle Chanel's father, who often traveled around without his family and had many love relationship with other women, left the family by leaving children in orphanages.

During six years in the orphanage of Roman Catholic monastery of Aubazine, Gabrielle Chanel learned the trade of a seamstress. She was famous in the orphanage because she made beautiful dress for friends' dolls. When she reached eighteen, she decided to go to Notre Dame, a convent boarding school in Moulins as a charity case. However, the life of Notre Dame was not as attractive as it seemed on the outside. "Discipline was strict and the differences between the rich and the poor were put sharply in focus; forced to stay apart from the paying students, Gabrielle Chanel and other indigent girls lived in unheated quarters, sat separately in class, ate inferior food and dressed in plainer, rougher clothing" (Wallach 6). However, even in this harsh environment, Gabrielle Chanel did not lose her pride and elegance. Humiliated by her poverty, Gabrielle Chanel tried even more to observe rich students' behavior and language by comparing them to those of poor students and acted just like one of them. "Pride was the key to her character, and it burst through her eyes, her nose, her gustures, and her actions" (Wallach 6). The life at Notre Dame did not give only the idea of rich life to Gabrielle Chanel, but also the tailoring skills and experiences. "She learned to sew at the boarding school, and her first job was that of a shop girl for A Sainte-Marie, a lingerie and trousseau firm in Moulins" and "a tailor, mending the uniforms of the army officers stationed in the garrison town" (Wallach 6).

With "dreams of fortune and even adoration filled her monotonous days tailing in the shops," Gabrielle Chanel performed as a cabaret singer in a popular Moulins cabaret (Wallach 9). At the clubs, she was called "Coco." "Coco" was a nickname that Alber Chanel, Gabrielle Chanel's father, gave to Gabrielle Chanel when she was young. During this time period,

Gabrielle Chanel lacked competent singing skill, but "Gabrielle possessed a generous ability to flirt" (Wallach 10). With her flirtation, Gabrielle Chanel met rich, young French textile heir Étienne Balsan in the cabaret. Balsan was "a cavalry officer whose family fortune came from manufacturing textiles" (Wallach 10). Balsan impressed on Chanel the beauties of rich life styles. As Étienne Balsan asked Chanel to join him at Royallieu, Gabrielle Chanel actually met people in high society and directly experienced wealthy life. At Royallieu, "where nobles and heirs such as Baron de Roy or Léon de Laborde or Balsan's brother Jacques often arrived with at least one young woman on the arm," Chanel finally gained entry into wealthy life. At first, Chanel was amused with the wealthy environment around her and the clear contrast with other women of full shape with high leveled dresses. However, still she was determined not to be outdone like she was in Notre Dame. Her gifted talents started to show up as she drew some attention with her hats in Royallieu.

Chanel began to design hats as a hobby, which soon became a great interest of hers. "Instead of the heavily feathered or flowered spheres of great height and enormous width, Chanel used smaller, less complex frames and embellished them with only a tough of blossoms of plumes" (Wallach 17). This simple look struck several other mistresses of Balsan. "The actress Gabrielle Dorziat and the opera singer Marthe Davelli asked if she (Gabrielle Chanel) would do up some styles for them" (Wallach 17). With this hat business, Chanel's actual fashion business and reputation started within high society. In 1910, Gabrielle Chanel became a licensed modiste and opened her first boutique at 21 Rue Cambon, Paris named *Chanel Modes*. Also, in 1910, Chanel left Balsan. In 1912, Gabrielle Chanel's design boomed as theatre actress Gabrielle Dorizat modelled her hats in the F Noziere's play, *Bel Ami*. "As other designers followed her styles and the smaller hat became more fashionable, Chanel was recognized as an important hat designer" (Wallach 17).

During this busy time, in 1912, Chanel met Arthur "Boy" Capel at Pau. "His British background was blurred, but his ability to make money and friends was clear. By the age of thirty his intelligence and shrewd sense for business had earned him a fortune in shipping and coal" (Wallach 18). Arthur "Boy" Chapel had similar appearance with Chanel's father's look, who Chanel once admired for his carefree nature. Gabrielle Chanel praised him for "his penetrating eyes, thick black hair, and broad mustache" (Wallach 17). With her experienced charms, Arthur "Boy" Capel became one of her lovers. Like Balsan, Capel, also, helped Chanel to be recognizable to the public. Whenever, Chanel and Capel went to restaurants, "she (Chanel) wore distinctive hats and peculiar dresses" and this interesting scene created lots of gossip, which increased the fame of Chanel's new style and reputation of Chanel herself (Wallach 21). With the popularity of her hats, Chanel also popularized short hair for women. Furthermore, "despite her churlish attitude, her success with Capel clearly intrigued the women. Even though her prices were high, her spare, young style was appealing" (Wallach 22). Therefore, with the fame of her hat business and the relationship with Capel, in 1913, Gabrielle Chanel established new boutique in the fashionable seaside town, Deauville. In this new boutique, Gabrielle Chanel established luxurious casual clothes that were suitable for leisure and sport. The discomfort in Paris for too much public attention and gossip disappeared in Deauville. And in Deauville, Gabrielle Chanel created another new look in fashion.

Because of Deauville's cold weather, Chanel tried hard to keep warm. "To ward off a chill one day, she did as she often had done in the past and plucked a sweater from Boy. But instead of pulling it over her head, to keep it from messing her clothes she took her scissors and snipped it down the front, finished off the raw edge with ribbon and adding a collar and bow" (Wallach 25). Chanel revolutionized women's fashion with her straight, simple, uncorseted, and, above all, comfortable "Chanel Look." Practicality drove her style. The hand-knitted fabric was far thinner than the heavy embroideries or fancy taffetas, which was popular at that time (Wallach 25). Chanel's jersey was fluid and soft and moved as she did, allowing her body the kind of freedom she loved. This new jersey style struck other women, and it soon became Chanel's another fortune. Chanel once stated that "my fortune was founded on that old jersey just because I was so cold in Deauville" to author Paul

Morand (Wallach 25). With the start of Chanel's new jersey design, Chanel started to boom in her clothes line, too. By growing popularity of Chanel's line, in 1915, Chanel publicly launched her career as fashion designer throughout Europe, not just in Royallieu, with her next boutique called Chanel-Biarritz. "It was located near the Spanish border, and provide a convenient shopping stop for visitors … from neutral Spain" (Wallach 28). By its location, Chanel could spread her name in both sides of the Atlantic. "The American magazine *Harper's Bazaar* Showed ' a charming chemise,' one of the outfits form the Biarritz collection, and American *Vogue* soon followed with more spreads" (Wallach 28). Still, she did not stop her creative new ideas. In Paris, as the World War I began, women could not hire their drivers to take them shopping at rainy days. Therefore, "Chanel invented a rubberized style based on the lines of a chauffeur's coat, with deep pockets and adjustable tabs at the cuffs (Wallach 29). This new "invention" was bought by customers "from North America to Argentina, from England to Russia" (Wallach 29). By 1915, Chanel was becoming the leading example of the new woman. Slim, narrow-hipped and nearly breastless, she had shed her corsets, shortened her skirts, cut her long hair and allowed her youthful face to tan in the sun (Wallach 28).

However, unlike her sharply growing fashion business, her love relationship did not worked out as Gabrielle Chanel wished. As Capel took a trip to London for his business, Capel met his fiancée, Diana Wyndham, a daughter of a British lord. Then, toward the end of the war, Capel announced his plan to marry. This displeased Chanel, but Chanel had known the incompleteness in their relationship since "Capel was a man on the rise, and she had neither the class nor the wealth to help him" (Wallach 29). However, even after Capel's marriage, Capel and Chanel continued to have relationship. But, their relationship finally ended in Capel's death by the car accident. Janet Wallach, the author of *Chanel: Her Style and Her Life*, stated that "She would never love another man as much as she had loved Capel" because through Capel, Chanel experienced "a feast of loving and being loved" (Wallach 30 – 31). Therefore, feeling isolated and despondent, Chanel doubled her effort at her work. But, the greater tragedy followed after the news about Capel's death in the automobile accident. From the heartbreaking death of Arthur Capel, Chanel fell into a breakdown. She asked her butlers and her friends to change her room into complete blackness. In order to cheer up her friend, Misia Sert, a Polish pianist who was one of Chanel's closest friends, brought Chanel to a luxurious ball where all famous artists and rich people gathered. At the ball, everyone looked down at Chanel, even though Chanel had been begged to attend that party only two years before. This belittlement hurt Chanel's pride and stirred Chanel to focus on her work again.

Then, in May 1921, through Masia, Gabrielle Chanel met a famous Russian composer, Igor Stravinsky, "who had spent the war years in Switzerland with his wife, Catherine Nossenko, and their two daughters" (Madsen 109). Since Stravinsky's family did not have a place to stay in France, Chanel invited them to stay in her villa. Then, again, like all other men who became enthralled with Chanel's independent pride, Stravinsky naturally fell to Chanel's charming talents and pride. They had several love relationships, but Chanel was not in love. To Chanel, the relationship between Igor Stravinsky and Gabrielle Chanel was just a great benefit for each other. For Igor Stravinsky who lost everything in the Russian Revolution of 1917, Chanel's generous offer to "subsidize a revival of *The Rite*" was a new start for Igor Stravinsky. And for Gabrielle Chanel, it was a considerable social coup for Chanel to act as benefactor to such a celebrated musician. In addition, Chanel invented her most well-known perfume, No. 5, while Stravinsky lived with Chanel, which proved the powerful influences between them. However, their beneficial relationship ended when Igor Stravinsky decided to propose to Chanel to marry him. Chanel "loved men. She could not stand the idea of not being loved in return, but hated being dependent on any man, falling prey to anyone" (Madsen 121). Therefore, knowing the seriousness of their relationship, Chanel had to leave Stravinsky.

However, still, Chanel's business did not stop there. Gabrielle Chanel's sense of smell was as acute as her sense of fashion. Chanel stated that "of all the human senses, smell is the most perfect" (Bott 153). "She believed the droplets of 'smell good' that a woman daubed behind an ear, in the hollow of a shoulder, on the back of the wrist were mandatory" (Madsen 132). And Chanel's sharp sense of smell was shown in 1921 by her first perfume, Chanel No. 5. It was a huge hit. From the start of its first launch, it continuously remained as, even until today, one of the bestselling perfumes in the world. "Chanel No. 5, the first 'modern perfume' or 'abstract fragrance,' is ageless" (Bott 153). No single essence stands out, but its aura remains unique and recognizable. Chanel No. 5's mysterious, but significant scent attracted many women. Almost instantly, Chanel's Chanel No.5 perfume enhanced Chanel's name around the world. It boosts Chanel's business and her name as top designer.

Then, in Tuesday, October 29, 1929, Wall Street stock market crash, which is known as the "Black Tuesday," hit the economy of the United States. But, it took a year to cross the Atlantic, and, on June 1930, the recession finally reached Europe. As soon as the recession hit Europe, it affected the luxury trade. "By 1931, it was considered bad taste to even *look* rich" (Madsen 181). This new trend affected Chanel's business, since Chanel couture was the most expensive in Paris by this period. In order to keep the cost low, "in her collection for the spring of 1931, she included thirty-five cotton evening dresses in piqué, lace, organdy, net,… and zipper" (Madsen 181). Still, Chanel could not bring back the customers. Then, in 1931, she moved to America to work for the movies. Through Misia, Chanel had met "Samuel Goldwyn, the maddeningly self-centered movie mogul who … was convinced people wanted to keep their minds off the Depression" (Madsen 182) through glamorous or thrilling movies. Samuel Goldwyn believed that Chanel was necessary to upgrade Hollywood's fashion status. At first, Chanel hesitated to work with Goldwyn because Goldwyn's offer seemed to be "someone from the market squares of her childhood, another rube and wily cardsharp" (Madsen 182). But, finally Chanel accepted Goldwyn's offer to work on his film's wardrobe when Goldwyn asked Chanel to just visit Hollywood and see what pictures had to offer her. At Hollywood, Chanel met several top film directors and managers, and saw how films were shot. However, as Chanel saw the progress, Chanel felt that studio is ruthless and indifferent. Chanel commented "the stars are the producers' servants" (Madsen 190). And this image made Chanel to get back to her own business. On the way back Paris, in 1933, after two years of organizing Goldwyn's Hollywood fashion, Gabrielle Chanel stopped by New York. For Chanel, New York was more fascinating and productive. Chanel discovered New York's fashion as business. Chanel found out that, in Klein's, the discount bazaar on Union Square, "dresses that sold on Fifth Avenue for twenty dollars were priced at four dollars in this discount emporium" (Madsen 191). Chanel recognized that some of Klein's dresses plagiarized Chanel's design, but "she decided that it was hopeless to try and fight it, that piracy was the flattering result of success" (Madsen 191).

At Paris, with deepening Depression, many designers closed their businesses. But, fortunately, Chanel could hold on to her business with the financial support from the two years of designing in Hollywood. Also, Chanel's work in Hollywood augmented her name in Paris. "*Vogue* announced that Chanel had revolutionized Hollywood by dressing Ina Claire in the simplest of white satin pajamas" (Madsen 195). Still, Chanel was determined to use real jewels. However, instead of using cheap jewels, Chanel made multipurpose accessories to attract more clients. "All her more elaborate pieces could be taken apart: The tiaras turned into bracelets, the eardrops into brooches, the stars into buckles" (Madsen 196). And Chanel mixed real and fake jewels to lower the prices. With her unique, but pragmatic method, Chanel safely survived during the Depression.

Still, even with her well running business, Gabrielle Chanel faced another problem: workers' strike. At the polls of 1936, by workers, "the advent of the Front Popularire was welcomed by the masses as a thrilling victory promising long-overdue social and economic reforms and by a terrified right as bringing the country to the brink of communism" (Madsen 213). Workers, who feared that the victory at the polls might be snatched from them, wanted Front Populaire to immediately fulfill "its promises of paid vacation, extended family support, unemployment insurance, and a forty-hour work week" (Madsen 214). In order to press their demand, many workers, over the nation, went on strikes, and Chanel's workers were not exceptions. On June, 1936, Chanel's workers went on sit-down strikes in front of Chanel's Rue Cambon boutique. The scene of the group of her workers made Chanel dumbfounded. "The House of Chanel was one of the trade's best managed in an industry where turmoil was a tradition" (Madsen 215). At first, Chanel was furious at her workers' proposals, but, with her lawyer, Premier Blum, the starter of Popular Front government, Chanel and her workers made compromises: "no reprisals, wage increases ranging from 7 to 15 percent, the right of collective bargaining, the right to unionize, a forty-hour work week, and an annual two-week paid vacation" (Madsen 216). Chanel knew that she needed to settled the strike by the end of July, in order to prepare fall-winter collection perfectly, since her rivals, like Schiaparelli, already settled down their workers and worked on their next collection. Therefore, Chanel swallowed her pride. However, still, Chanel did not forgive them. "Decades later, she would rail against the 'madness' of 1936" (Madsen 217). Still, even with the "madness of 1936," "no fashion designer has ever stood still, or yet retained client loyalty" like Chanel did (Madsen 218). Chanel was on top of the fashion world. However, Chanel concerned that she was might out of luck. And presses' more interest in Schiaparelli's collection, in 1935, deepened Chanel's worries. Also, in 1930s, Chanel faced several new rivals. Cristóbal Balenciaga, a Spaniard who created dresses for royalty and celebrities, was one of newly rising fashion designers. His designs were "beautiful but austere in spite of their richness" (Madsen 219). Chanel's another rival was Lucien Lelong. Pierre Blamain and Christian Dior were his collaborators. He was not a best designer, but "woman felt secure wearing his clothes" (Madsen 220). Chanel's unstable faith continued through the end of 1930s with the likely coming war. In 1939, most designers foresaw the coming war and talked about useful looks as a coming trend. However, ironically, the collection of 1939 was called "a hymn to innocence" (Madsen 226). But, then, the World War II overshadowed the collection shows. As the war approaches and the power of Germany expanded rapidly, many men and women were gathered for the war. And Chanel at Rue Cambon, after three weeks when Britain and France finally declared war on Germany in response to Hilter's invasion of Poland, closed the House of Chanel without notice to her staff.

Only the perfume boutique remained open. Her workers and the government tried to stop her because the high fashion for troops might boost soldiers' morale. Some said Chanel felt "eclipsed by Schiaparelli" (Madsen 229). Still, Chanel was convinced that it was not a period for fashion. During the World War II, Chanel lived in the Hotel Ritz Paris, and this lifestyle continued on and off for more than 30 years, making the hotel her Paris home even during the German occupation. And during this period, Chanel had an affair with a Nazi officer, so Chanel faced some years of diminished popularity and an exile of sorts to Switzerland from 1945 to 1953.

Therefore, Chanel did not open her boutique again until 1954. In 1953, Chanel made a gown, "a dress cut from one huge curtain of crimson taffeta" (Madsen 282), for one of the most important parties of 1953. At the ball, everyone asked who the designer of Chanel's gown was. This massive compliments and interest made Chanel to start her business again. At seventy, in 1954, Chanel was still bold and proud. And she still determined to strengthen the bases of her classic line. The industry was different from the time Chanel closed her boutique in 1939. "From the basic silk, wool, and cotton available when Chanel started before World War I, dozens of alternatives – grease-resistant, permanently pleated, glazed, shrinkproof, waterproof, washable – were coming on the market" (Madsen 282). Chanel wanted to be on the lead of the new movement. Her only store in 31 Rue Cambon, which had been selling the perfume only, was reopened again. As her second coming was approaching to show in public, "she wrestled with each costume. She pulled apart and pinned together again, shortening, lengthening, denuding, touching up, all to pare down to the function and logic of the body" (Madsen 286). However, her previous plan to have 130 model for the new collection was almost impossible, so Chanel moved the collection to February 5th,1954. And the show began.

> *A photographer caught her (Chanel) on top of the stairs, in her white chemise, black silk vest, and severe skirt, mutely looking down. The mannequins, with bows at the back of their heads, came out six steps apart until there were*

often seven or eight of them at once, each reflected in the mirrored walls until the room overflowed with feminine allure. The tall models walked slowly, the small rounded ones walked faster. The presentation was quaint. Buyers, journalists, and fashion devotees... saw the models enter, pose, pause for an editor in the front row to feel the fabric, pose against, turn slowly – all the while carrying a numbered card in one hand. (Madsen 288)

It was not like any trend of the collection at this time period. Everyone "had grown used to the zip of Dior's shows, where models came out moving quickly, outfitted with handbags, gloves, and even umbrellas" (Madsen 288). Right after the show, the news of failure of Chanel's new coming spread throughout the world. All the press publicized that Chanel's sense was not sharp as it had been in 1930s, and her collection was out-of-date. As a seventy year woman, Chanel was exhausted with all her diligent work, but more than exhaustion, she was disappointed. However, still, Chanel moved on to her next collection. She admitted she was disappointed, but she wanted "to go on, go on, and win" (Madsen 289). Then, with the financial help from Chanel's lover, Pierre Wertheimer, who was in the Parfums Chanel board, Chanel continued her work. Then, after three weeks, along with the fame of Chanel's perfume, Chanel started to get fame from America. *Life* magazine said that "Chanel, 'the name behind the most famous perfumes in the world,' had lost none of her prewar skills" (Madsen 290). "Women found the pared-down Chanel silhouette young and easygoing in ways that were more truly modern than Dior's careful sophistication and Balenciaga's sculptural formality" (Madsen 291).

The revolutionary 1960s was all about minimalism. However, still, Chanel insisted to keep her "Chanel Look" – "the short, straight, collarless jacket, the slightly flaring skirt, and hems that never budged from mid-knee" (Madsen 300). She criticized women who were over thirty wearing miniskirts. Still, many women loved Chanel. "Mrs. Kennedy had worn a Chanel suit for her visit to Dallas on November 22, 1963" (Madsen 300).

She never lost the faith in her sense of fashion and she worked hard. Even with all days and nights work, Chanel seemed ironically get stronger and stronger.

Then, in 1962, with her great fame as a successful designer, Chanel was offered to make a movie about her life. Frederick Brisson, a Broadway producer, asked Chanel to sell her story for his next musical. With Chanel's comeback in 1954, Frederick Brisson wanted to create a musical about Chanel's life. At first, acquaintances of Brisson warned Brisson to talk about the musical to Chanel's lover, Wertheimer. However, when Chanel heard about the news Wertheimer rejected Brisson for having a musical about her story without telling her, Chanel persisted to Wertheimer that she has the right for her own life. Therefore, Chanel finally confirmed to allow Brisson to make a musical about her life named *Coco*. However, Chanel only accepted Brisson to portray her youth life during 1920s to 1930s.

Even with the musical, Chanel devoted all her time working on her next collection in her couture house. "She hated Sundays when she couldn't cross Rue Cambon and work herself into a stupor on collection preparations" (Madsen 316). However, her health could not follow her passion. Therefore, she hired Francois Mironnet as her manservant and her caretaker. Like all men Chanel had passed, Francois Mironnet became close companion for Chanel. Chanel suffered from insomnia, too. Still, her falling health did not stop her from fashion. She still spent most of her time at her boutique and hated Sundays and Hollidays because she could not work on her designs. Even the day she died, Sunday, January 10, 1971, she was looking forward to going back to work on the next day. On Sunday, Chanel took a ride with Claude Baillén to the chauffeured Cadillac. Then, after the ride, she slept a little. When she woke up, she suddenly could not breathe. Céline, Chanel's maid, tried to open the window and hoisted up Chanel's dress. But it was too late. Chanel closed her eyes with words, "You see, this is how you die" (Madsen 328). Chanel died at the age of eighty-seven.

Gabrielle Coco Chanel, a poor orphanage girl, became "a self-made millionaire and founder of the first fashion empire, she had captured the admiration of millions of women around the world and captivated dozens of men, among them some of the richest, most powerful, most gifted, most famous in Europe" (Wallach 2). Even though she lived openly with a man she loved, she never married anyone and enjoyed financial independence as an entrepreneur with a flourishing business. The massive production quickened the entire fashion tempo. In order to have such an honored name, Chanel faced several problems and tragic loses. One of Brisson's acquaintances, Alan Jay Lerner once stated that Chanel was "a woman who sacrifices everything for her independence and who realizes loneliness is the price she has to pay" (Madsen 314). Yet it was above all an attitude that she imparted, and that women still want now, and it has made Chanel style span nearly a century. Passionate, focused and fiercely independent, Chanel was a virtual tour de force.

Bibliography

Karbo, Karen. *The Gospel According to Coco Chanel*. Guilford, CT: Skirt. 2009.

Wallach, Janet. *Chanel: Her Story and Her Life*. New York: Nan A. Talese. 1998.

Gaines, Ann. *Coco Chanel*. Philadelphia: Chelsea House. 2004.

Madsen, Axel. *Chanel: A Woman of Her Own*. New York: Henry Hol and Company. 1990.

Bott, Daniéle. *Chanel: Collections and Creations*. New York: Thames& Hudson. 2007.

"How Did Benjamin Franklin Become a Major Leader in America?"

Martin Kim
Northern Highlands Regional High School

Benjamin Franklin (January 17, 1706 – April 17 1790), one of the most well-known Founding Fathers of the United States, had many successful careers in his life. He became a great leader in his careers as a printer, scientist, inventor, civic activist, and diplomat. When Benjamin worked as a printer, he had once been a librarian and postmaster general of Philadelphia. His great start and accomplishments led to different careers and helped him to be almost the most famous 18th century American.

Benjamin Franklin was born on Milk Street in Boston, on January 6, 1706. He was the youngest son of five generations of youngest sons (p.8, Clark). Benjamin had nine siblings, seven half siblings, a soap maker father named Josiah Franklin, and mother named Abiah Folger. Benjamin's father, Josiah Franklin had married twice; seven children were from his first wife, Anne's children and the other ten, include Benjamin were from his second wife, Abiah's children (p.11, Clark). Since there were too many children in Franklin's family, it was difficult for Ben's father to give every child enough education. However, luckily, Ben could go to South Grammar and George Brownell's school for a few years. Since his father had taken care of Ben's education, maybe Ben was one of the most educated in his family.

The main reason why Ben's father wanted his son to receive a lot of education was that he wanted Ben to be a clergy man. "It was with the ministry in view that Benjamin junior was sent to Boston's Latin School. The aim of life here was to train pupils in the use of sufficient Latin to pass into Harvard, the next and almost inevitable step along the path of theological progress in the Boston of those days" (p.12, Clark). Because Josiah Franklin had many sons, he felt that he should make at least one of them a clergy man. "His father had early decided that this child should become a minister, the family's tithe to the church" (p.11, Clark). Thus, Josiah singled out Ben to be the son who receives the most education.

When Ben realized that he wasn't able get more education because his family was way too poor for giving children enough education, he started to work after he had finished going to school in 1716. "But it soon became clear that the cost of education, especially of a college education, would far outrun the family's means" (p.6, Gaustad). Before Ben had become a printer, he tried to work as a tradesman because of his father's recommendation. Ben's father usually recommended Ben to become what he wanted. However, since Ben loved to read and write, he decided to work as an apprentice of his half – brother, James Franklin. James Franklin was Josiah and Anne's son who was a printer in Boston. Working as an apprentice of James, Ben usually had some problems with James because they couldn't cooperate with each other. Once, Ben was afraid that James would not publish his article because he was so young; he slipped the article under the door when the office was closed. The next day, his brother found the article, discussed it with news people and praised it. James published in the newspaper with a note saying that an article from this writer is welcome; Ben was thrilled (p.27, Zall). This series of essay that Ben had written was under the pseudonym, Silence Dogood.

Ben's apprenticeship under his brother was very important to his development as a leader.

> *The New England Courant* was important to Benjamin Franklin's development in at least three different ways. It brought him into touch with practicing writers, notably Nathaniel Gardner, who wrote regularly for the paper, and

> has been called 'perhaps the greatest single influence upon [his] prose style.' It gave him an insight into the mechanics of journalism and particularly of pamphleteering journalism. Even afterward, when it became expedient to persuade the public to support one cause or oppose another, Franklin would know how to phrase the argument, present the facts – or at least those favorable to his cause – and package his case in words that would persuade the ordinary reader. Possibly as important, the experience of *The New England Courant* gave him an apprenticeship in opposing authority, an occupation which he thoroughly enjoyed and in whose practice he became a skilled operator (p.18, Clark).

Thus, Ben's printer experience was to shade the rest of his life. *The New England Courant*, in James's paper became very popular, but it made fun of Boston society. In 1722, James was put in prison twice because of the essay. "James Franklin was summoned before the Governor's Council, and for printing what was alleged to be a sentence critical of the authorities, was sentenced to prison for a month (p.22, Clark). On his release, moreover, it was ordered that 'James Franklin should no longer print the paper called the *New England Courant*'" (p.22, Clark). After James retuned from prison, he argued with Ben several times. James was starting to realize that Ben was working too well and was kind of a threat to him. Ben finally decided to leave James's workshop and tried to find other printer workshops in Boston but James had secretly told all printers in Boston not to hire Ben (p.23, Clark).

However, Ben never gave up on finding a job in Boston and left his hometown to find a new work place on September 25, 1723. Benjamin's new life started full of solitude because he had nothing on him in New York, an unfamiliar city where he first went to find a new job. Moreover, he couldn't find any job in there and had to travel even farther from his hometown. He was homeless and nearly penniless when he reached Philadelphia, which was known as the biggest city in America at that time. (p.75, Labaree). "I was dirty by tumbling about from my Journey; my Pockets were stuff'd out with Shirts & Stockings; I knew no Soul, nor where to look for Lodging, and I was very hungry, and my whole Stock of cash consisted of a Dutch Dollar and about a Shilling in Copper" (p.36, Zall). Fortunately, Benjamin found Samuel Keimer's printer shop with help of a Quaker named Bradford. Also, he became a lodger at John and Sarah Read's house in 1723, where he met his wife, Deborah Read. Deborah was John and Sarah's daughter who first married a man named John Rogers while Benjamin was gone to England for a few years. However, there was a rumor that Rogers already had a wife in England. "When did so, in the autumn of 1726, it was to find that Deborah had married during his absence. Her husband was a Mr. Rogers. But to the fact that Mr. Rogers had disappeared soon after the marriage there were added two suggestions: one was that he already had a wife at the time of his marriage to Deborah Read; the other that he had died shortly after his disappearance" (p.42, Clark). On November 5, 1724, Benjamin went to England for the first time to get some supplies he would need to start his own printing shop. He was able to go to England because Pennsylvania governor, William Keith, had promised him to help him with the finance. Even though Benjamin's father denied giving help to Benjamin to open his own printer shop, Keith had promised Benjamin that he would help with everything that Benjamin needs (p.19, Gaustad).

But, when Benjamin arrived in London in 1724, he was left alone with nothing again, like when he first settled in Philadelphia; he realized that he came to London just to find out that Keith had broken the promise. "He 'let me into Keith's Character, told me there was not the least Probability that he had written any Letters for me, that no one who knew him had the smallest Dependence on him, and he laught at the Notion of the Governor's giving me a Letter of Credit, having as he said no Credit to give.' Denham was right. There were no letters" (p.26, Clark). Benjamin was first hopeless but soon, found a job in London and started to work with a Quaker named Thomas Denham who told Benjamin about Keith's unreliable promise. Regarding this period, Benjamin says, "I was surprised to find these were not the governor's letters; and, after recollecting and comparing circumstances, I began to doubt his sincerity. I found my friend Denham, and opened the whole affair to him" (p.35, Conn). Afterward, Benjamin came back to America with Denham on July 23, 1726, and quickly learned business from Denham. "Clerking for Thomas Denham would prove an excellent school of business ethics, for his mentor exemplified the Quaker virtues of honesty, hard work, thrift, prudence, and others now associated with liberal capitalism – especially the notion that honesty is good for business and good business positions one to do good works for humanity, an idea underpinning Franklin's career" (p.79, Zall). However, Benjamin and Denham both fell ill with pleurisy, and Denham died. With no choice left, Benjamin returned to his old job at Samuel Keimer's work shop (p.21, Gaustad).

In 1728, Benjamin and his business partner, James Meredith started their business with James's loan from his parents. They became very successful and even bought Keimer's paper when Keimer went to bankruptcy; in 1729, Benjamin turned *the Pennsylvania Gazette* into the most successful newspaper in America with the first political cartoons on it. Later, Benjamin bought out his partner and became the most successful printer in town. After he saw some success, Benjamin began publishing *Poor Richard's Almanack* on December 28, 1732, under a pseudonym, Richard Saunders. *Poor Richard's Almanack* didn't only contain poems, calendars and predictions like weather reports, but it also contained Benjamin's great writings and creative quotes about saving money. "Published under the pseudonym of Richard Saunders, Franklin's very popular *Almanack* was filled with useful information such as tides, temperatures, and times for the rising and setting of the sun and moon, as well as witty epigrams" (p.27, Gaustad).

On September 1, 1730, Benjamin Franklin and Deborah Read married in a common–law marriage because of the fear that Rogers might reappear. They raised Benjamin's illegitimate son William, who had become a governor of New Jersey at his forty's. "It is to this same son, William Franklin, that the Autobiography is ostensibly addressed. William Franklin was at that time the forty-year-old Royal Governor of New Jersey, a patronage job acquired nine years earlier when his father's relation to the ministry was more comfortable and the ministry hoped to inspire the father's gratitude" (p.16, Seavey). Deborah gave a birth to a boy named Francis Folger Franklin, but he died because of smallpox when he was only four years old in 1736. The second child was a daughter named Sarah, born in 1743, who later gave great care to Benjamin when he returned from France in 1785. Even though Deborah was likely to be a domestic woman, she managed many businesses when Benjamin was busy running print, government and many other businesses. (p.265, Clark). Deborah Franklin was a great wife to Benjamin, but she couldn't live a great life with Benjamin as a family; Benjamin and Deborah lived apart from each other for more than ten years because of Benjamin's political career. "Before they were complete he heard, on February 20, that his wife, Deborah, had died of paralysis two months earlier. It was eleven years before that he had left her, expecting, or at least claiming to expect, that they would be parted only for a year or so at the most. In 1768, she had suffered a partial palsy of the tongue and had begun to lose her memory. Her doctor, Thomas Bond, warned Franklin that although she had recovered, her constitution seemed impaired" (p.265, Clark). "Deborah must have considered the possibility that her husband had decided to stay in England without her, while merely holding out promises of his return to Philadelphia. As late as 1773, several years after she had begun to fail physically, Franklin was using 'Prudential Algebra' in London to decide whether he should go home or remain in England. There was nothing in his algebraic formula about wife, family, and friends back home" (p.19, Morgan). "Franklin's feelings for his wife have remained something of an enigma. On her part, there was regret at his continued absence but a loyal resignation to put up with it" (p.265, Clark).

Before Benjamin was involved in political career, he was involved in civic improvement in 1727 by organizing *the Junto* which was a club that led tradesmen like Benjamin to meet once a week and plan for civic improvements. "[In the autumn I] form'd most of my ingenious Acquaintance into a Club, which we call'd the Junto. We met every Friday Evening. The Rules I drew up, requir'd that every Member in his Turn should produce one or more Queries on any Point of Morals, Politics or Natural Philosophy, to be discuss'd by the Company, and that every once in three Months produce and read an Essay of his own Writing on any Subject he pleas'd" (p.85, Zall). In 1731, with assiduous work on his job, Benjamin became the first president of America's first public library called the "Library Company of Philadelphia." (p.50, Clark). Then in 1737, he became Postmaster General of Philadelphia. When Benjamin was working at the public library, the library received an account of the new German Experiments in Electricity from F.R.S. of London, Peter Collinson. Benjamin's careers as a scientist and an inventor started here because he felt curious about the subject since the nature of electricity was very little known at that time. Surprisingly, Benjamin's unique experiment was succeed and impressed Europeans who thought that Americans were not sophisticated.

> In France, the surprise was increased by the background of the man who had proposed the experiment. Dalibard's 'Mr. Franklin' was not a Frenchman. He did not come from England or from Germany. He was in fact, a Colonial from across the Atlantic, a man from that distant country on the edge of the wilderness where all effort, from what one heard, tended to concentrate on the problems of survival against the elements and the Indians rather than on the profundities of scientific research (p.4-5 Clark).

It is because Benjamin was able to impress Europeans, especially the French, that Benjamin was able later to play the role of diplomat in Europe. After Benjamin had observed for lightening with his kite experiment, he invented swim fins, a musical instrument, and bifocals in 1736. "It is true that the Franklin stove is the best-known spinoff from his nonelectrical work; it is true that he is apt to be recalled as the inventor of bifocal glasses and of a multiplicity of gadgets" (p.53, Clark).

In the same year, he had done many other accomplishments other than inventing; he was involved in many kinds of civic improvements in Philadelphia such as starting a city hospital in 1751. He helped to organize the first police force and volunteer firefighting companies in America, called the Union Fire Company. "Other companies were formed in Philadelphia, and Franklin was eventually able to claim that the city had the best fire services in the world" (p.52, Clark). Later that year, he had done some more work for civic improvement "The city soon paved its streets, lit them by gas (with an improved lamp globe design contributed by Franklin), and cleaned them on a regular schedule. Franklin was involved in so much civic improvement that when one citizen proposed the building of a hospital, potential donors held back until they learned Franklin's opinion of the project" (p.36, Gaustad).

In 1748, Benjamin got involved in politics quickly and became a councilman after he had retired from his job as a printer. "To Americans, Benjamin Franklin is the epitome of all that America should be the patriot as responsible as Washington for prizing the young Colonies from the grip of the British, the successful businessman as well as that rare bird, the honest politician" (p.6, Clark). Since Benjamin became wealthy enough to retire from his job, he gave his printing business to his business partner named David Hall. Benjamin started to have more interest on public affairs and politics later and was once appointed as a president of the Academy and College of Philadelphia (p.145, Clark). After the academy opened on November 13, 1749, it was merged with the University of the State of Pennsylvania to become the University of Pennsylvania. Furthermore, Benjamin was elected to the Pennsylvania Assembly in 1736 and became a Justice of the Peace for Philadelphia in 1751, which made him responsible for enforcing laws (p.57, Clark). He also was appointed joint deputy postmaster–general of North America in August 10, 1753. "Franklin solicited the deputy postmaster generalship in May 1751; he and Hunter were commissioned on Aug. 10, 1753, and before the end of that year issued detailed instructions to postmasters in North America" (p.208, Larabee). In his autobiography, Benjamin said, "Having been for some time employed by the Postmaster General of America, as his Comptroller, in regulating the several Offices, and bringing the

Officers to account, I was upon his Death in 1753 appointed jointly with Mr. William Hunter to succeed him, by a Commission from the Postmaster General in England" (p.208, Larabee).

As a deputy postmaster, Benjamin tried to protect Pennsylvania in many ways when the Indians tried to fight for their lands with French soldiers' support. Since the Indians were supported by the French soldiers, the entire colonies' frontier was in danger. "In 1754, War with France being again apprehended, a Congress of Commissioners from the different Colonies, was by an Order of the Lords of Trade, to be assembled at Albany, there to confer with the Chiefs of the Six Nations, concerning the Means of defending both their Country and ours. Governor Hamilton, having receiv'd this Order, acquainted the House with it, requesting they would furnish proper Presents for the Indians to be given on this Occasion; and naming the Speaker (Mr. Norris) and my self, to join Mr. Thomas Penn and Mr. Secretary Peters, as Commissioners to act for Pennsylvania" (p.209, Larabee). Not only to protect Pennsylvania but the entire colony, Benjamin thought of uniting and published an essay about the unification of the colonies in May 4, 1754. In his essay, contained a very famous political cartoon; a snake cut into pieces representing each colony with a caption "JOIN OR DIE" was published in newspapers. "In 1754 Franklin tried desperately to convince the colonies that they needed to join together for mutual defense against the French in the western frontier. Though he failed in this effort, the earnestness of his attempt is evident in the paragraph below, as in his first political cartoon – both published in the Pennsylvania Gazette of May 9, 1754" (p.68, Gautad).

In 1756, Benjamin organized the Pennsylvania militia to fight against the Native Americans' rebels. Later that year, Benjamin became colonel agent and was sent to England by Pennsylvania Assembly for Pennsylvania's state political influence. He planned to convince the British government to allow the Pennsylvania assembly to tax the colony's proprietors who lived in London and owned large amount of land in Pennsylvania (p.129-130, Clark). These proprietors had inherited most of their lands from William Penn, who was the founder of

Pennsylvania; these selfish proprietors, however, avoided to pay tax on their lands and didn't have any attempt to help the colony people. Benjamin became very frustrated when the most of the people in London didn't care about the colony, so he started to write essays and pamphlets about America. Benjamin had been working on his job with great efforts to persuade the British to let the proprietors pay the tax. Finally in 1760, with a series of arguments and meetings, Benjamin had succeeded his mission in London.

With a success on his work, Benjamin returned to Philadelphia in 1762 but soon found a problem with proprietors when a gang of young murderers known as "Paxton Boys" murdered many Christian Indians. "Presbyterian Irish from the township of Paxton murdered a group of peaceful Christian Indians in retaliation for the depredations committed by marauding tribes during the uprising known as Pontiac's War" (p.181, Fleming). Benjamin had become furious and denounced the "Paxton Boys" in a newspaper article and easily solved the problem, returning them from Philadelphia. Benjamin later attempted to give Pennsylvania a royal government, instead of keeping the proprietorship which made the most of the power to belong to the proprietors. However, Benjamin failed at this because he lost his governor election in October 1764. Failing in his attempt to make Pennsylvania a royal government, Benjamin noticed another problem, the British government's Stamp Act; colonists thought this was an unfair tax and were willing to fight against it. Benjamin also tried to prevent the British from passing this act in London by urging the king's ministers. Even with the colonists' complaints and Benjamin's urging, the Stamp Act was passed on February 17, 1765, and the Declaratory Act of 1766 asserted that the authority of the Stamp Act was unlimited (p.262, Larabee). However, Benjamin had noticed the Americans' deep resentment of the Stamp Act and started to testify against the Act. On February 13, 1766, Benjamin answered some of the Members of Parliament's questions including, "Whether the Americans would submit to the stamp duty if it were moderated?", "Was the temper of America had been toward Britain before 1763?", "What used to be the pride of the Americans?", and "What is now their pride?" (p.193, Clark).

Benjamin's significant answers to these questions helped overturn the Act in the end; for the most important question, he answered that the pride of the Americans was to indulge in the fashions and manufactures of Great Britain. After Benjamin's influenced work, the Stamp Act was finally repealed on March 18, 1766 (p.193, Clark). A few states were very impressed with Benjamin's success in dealing with Britain. Georgia appointed Benjamin as a representative in London on April 1768, and New Jersey and Massachusetts did the same in 1769 and in 1770 (p.200, Clark).

After the fight against the Stamp Act, many Americans considered Benjamin the great representative and an advocate in Britain. However, when the British's ignorance about the Americans never seemed to end, Benjamin wrote some essays, like "Rules By Which a Great Empire May Be Reduced to a Small One" in September 1773 (p.234-235, Clark). When anti-British in Massachusetts was increased, Benjamin wished the colonists to feel less angry about the British. Also, the governor of Massachusetts Thomas Hutchins and Lieutenant governor Andrew Oliver feared a revolt. Thus, the British government was asked to break the radicals. "It was known that the Hutchins letters had been written to Thomas Whately. But it was not known how they had come into the hands of whoever had sent them to Boston and it was not yet known that that person was Franklin, since Cushing, the fountainhead of the letters one they had arrived in Boston, had kept cautiously silent on this point" (p.237, Clark). Benjamin's falling from grace in both America and British started here. Benjamin somehow acquired the letter and sent them to the House of Representatives in Massachusetts. He had asked the House not to publish the letters, but it was leaked and the Colonies' anger toward the British grew even worse. Later, Benjamin was started to be known as a thief in London and removed from deputy postmaster general of North America in 1774 (pg.247, Clark). In early 1775, Benjamin had failed in the reconciliation of America and Britain and left Britain in January.

The Battle of Lexington and Concord broke out when Benjamin sailed back from London. "He had sailed from a country at peace; he landed in a country at war. During his weeks on the Atlantic the Colonies had gone through a series of traumatic experiences which were to change the world" (p.269, Clark). "When British reached Lexington the following morning they found a handful of Minutemen facing them" (pg.269, Clark). Benjamin, now a delegate to the Second Continental Congress, went on a mission to Canada to convince colonists to join the battle against Britain in March 1776. "He led a diplomatic mission to Canada through the ravages of an exceptionally hard winter and nearly succumbed to the effort" (p.272, Clark). Unfortunately, Benjamin failed to convince the colonists in Canada.

Back in Philadelphia, Benjamin had helped Thomas Jefferson with writing the Declaration of Independence from June 1776. "By that date Franklin had in fact been appointed – with Thomas Jefferson, John Adams, Roger Sherman of Connecticut and Robert R. Livingston of New York – to draw up a declaration that could be formally announced to the world" (p.285, Clark). "The Declaration of Independence was debated for nine hours in July 1, 1776, because Pennsylvania and South Carolina opposed it. However, the agreement finally came on July 4; two days later, it was published in the Pennsylvania Evening Post and on July 8, it was read in the State House yard before the Liberty Bell rung" (p.286, Clark).

In December 3, 1776, Benjamin was sent to France as a commissioner with Arthur Lee and Silas Deane; Benjamin's mission to France was known as his climax in his diplomatic career. "Some eighteen months were now to pass before Franklin left Philadelphia for the nine years in France which were to be the climax of his career" (pg. 271, Clark). Benjamin's work during a mission to France was probably the most successful work he had done in his entire life. "Much of Franklin's success in France was due to character, to a homely exterior which fascinated the sophisticated French court but concealed a high ability for intrigue. A great deal rested on his knowledge of American administration and also on the way in which the political game was played in Britain. But perhaps the most important factor in his success – which between 1777 and 1782 attracted some 26 million francs from the coffers of France into the service of the American Revolution – was the reputation he had acquired a quarter of a century earlier" (p.298, Clark).

When Americans won the Battle of Saratoga in 1777, Benjamin negotiated with the French government for an alliance. "There was the period which began with his first meeting with Vergennes and which ended – after the American victory over Burgoyne in the autumn of 1777 – with the signing of treaties between France and America, and , soon afterward, the formal outbreak of war between Britain and France" (p.317, Clark).

America, combined with French force, grew stronger enough to defeat British at the Battle of Yorktown. The war had been known as a minor skirmish against a handful of armed Colonial rebels in the summer of 1776. "By 1780, it had grown into a full-scale conflict against a formidable American army, a hornet's nest of privateers and the threatening military and naval forces of France" (p.370, Clark). A British army soon surrendered on October 19, 1781. "There then followed three and a half years of fluctuating encounters, ended by the British surrender at Yorktown in the closing weeks of 1781" (p.317, Clark). After the surrender, the British agreed to negotiate a peace treaty and finally the Americans signed the Treaty of Paris on September 3, 1783 which officially ended the Revolutionary War.

Benjamin Franklin, at the age of seventy-five, was sent to home on July 1785. Even though Benjamin was the eldest man in America at that time, he was elected as a president of Pennsylvania's supreme executive council and work for three years. "He was waited upon, moreover, by members of the Constitutional Society, and by the Anti-Constitutionalists, both of whom were to nominate him as a candidate in elections for the Supreme Executive Council the following month" (p.403, Clark). While he was the president of supreme executive council, Benjamin continued writing his *Autobiography* which he started in 1771.

In 1789, Benjamin was completely retired from all kinds of jobs. However, Benjamin petitioned the federal government to abolish slavery. "The previous month, Pennsylvania's antislavery organization had presented to the House of Representatives a petition for abolition, which Franklin had signed" (p.414, Clark). Until he became ill with pleurisy, Benjamin worked hard on abolishing slavery as much as what he had done for all other kinds of his careers. When Benjamin fell ill with pleurisy, his long life faced the end. "The end came when an abscess which had formed on a lung finally burst. 'The organs of respiration became gradually oppressed' his doctor wrote, 'a calm lethargic state succeeded and on the 17th [of April, 1790,] about eleven o'clock at night, he quietly expired, closing a long and useful life of eighty-four years and three months" (p.415, Clark). Benjamin Franklin, the genius who had liberated America, was mourned for three days on both sides of the Atlantic (p.415, Clark).

> *The early Colonists bred scientists other than Benjamin Franklin and men as deft politically. But his unusual combination of scientific flair and popular exposition revealed, particularly to France and to Britain, the intellectual potential already developed across the Atlantic. Returning to Europe in 1776 on the raft of his electrical reputation, old and plump yet still urged on by the mysterious impetus of genius, he had talked and intrigued, wheedled and borrowed, and helped to provide the troops in the field with the sinews of success. Franklin himself would have been among the first to agree that it was an admirable record (p.417, Clark).*

Bibliography

Clark, Ronald William, *Benjamin Franklin; A Biography*, New York: Random House, 1983.

Currey, Cecil B., *Road to Revolution Benjamin Franklin in England 1765-1775*; Anchor Books edition: 1968.

Gustad, Edwin S, *Benjamin Franklin*. New York: Oxford University Press, 2006.

Zall, Paul M., *Franklin on Franklin*. Kentucky: The University Press of Kentucky, 2000.

Houston, Alan, *Benjamin Franklin and the Politics of Improvement*. New York: Yale University Press, 2008.

Morgan, Edmund S., *The Autobiography of Benjamin Franklin*. Yale University Press, 1964.

Buxbaum, Melvin H., *Critical Essays on Benjamin Franklin*. Massachusetts: G..K. Hall & Co., 1987.

Wright, Esmond, *Benjamin Franklin; A Profile*. New York: Hill and Wang, 1970.

Labaree, Leonard W., *The Autobiography of Benjamin Franklin*. Yale University Press, 1964.

Granger, Bruce Ingham, Benjamin Franklin; An American Man of Letters. New York: Cornell University Press, 1964.

Barbour, Brian M., *Benjamin Franklin; A Collection of Critical Essays*. New Jersey: Prentice-Hall, 1979.

Fleming, Thomas, *The Fouding Fathers Benjamin Franklin; A Biography in His Own Words*. New York: Newsweek, Harper & Row 1972.

Pangle, Lorraine Smith, *The Political Philosophy of Benjamin Franklin*. Maryland: The Johns Hopkins University Press, 2007.

Towns, W. Stuart, *"We Want Our Freedon": Rhetoric of the Civil Rights Movement*. Praeger Publishers, 2002.

Kalter, Susan I., *Benjamin Franklin, Pennsylvania, and the First Nations*. Illinois: The Board of Trustees of the University of Illinois, 2006.

Walters, Kerry S., *Benjamin Franklin and His Gods*. Illinois: The Board of Trustees of the University of Illinois, 1999.

Seavy, Ormond, *Becoming Benjamin Franklin; The Autobiography and the Life*. Pennsylvania: The Pennsylvania State University Press, 1988.

Smythe Henry J. Jr., *The Amazing Benjamin Franklin*. New York: Frederick A. Stokes Company, 1929

Conn, Peter, *The Autobiography of Benjamin Franklin*. Pennsylvania: The Pennsylvania State University Press, 2005.

Morgan, David T., *The Devious Dr. Franklin, Colonial Agent: Benjamin Franklin's Years in London*. Georgia: Mercer University Press, 1996.

"An Inventor, a Teacher, and a Husband:
The Life and Challenges of Alexander Graham Bell"

Hoon Ho Jang
Ridgewood High School

"I then shouted into M [the mouthpiece] the following sentence: 'Mr. Watson – Come here – I want to see you.' To my delight he came and declared that he had heard and understood what I said."

- *Alexander Graham Bell, in his laboratory notebook on March 12, 1876 (Bruce, 181).*

The great success and fame of Alexander Graham Bell started when he uttered those words on March 10, 1876 (Pelta, 74). It was the first major breakthrough of his biggest invention, the telephone. In order to achieve the magnificent worldly fame he did, Alexander Graham Bell had to overcome many adversities in his life. Creating the telephone was just one of many challenges in Bell's life, but Alec triumphantly overcame these adversities to become a renowned inventor of the world, a devoted teacher of deaf children, and a loving husband of his one true love.

Alexander Bell's first of many adversities in his life was during his early childhood with his deaf mother. Born into a Scottish family that had enough money to live somewhat comfortably, Alexander Bell lived most of his youth in South Charlotte Street in Edinburgh. He was the second son of Melville and Eliza Bell. Eliza Grace Bell was deaf and no one could

114

communicate with her, except, Alexander, who found a way to communicate with his mother. Alec (or Aleck, for he had many nicknames) found a way to communicate with her by speaking in a low voice close to her forehead so she could feel the vibrations from the sound and "hear" what Alec was saying to her (Gray, 3). By overcoming his problem of not being able to communicate with his mother, Alec was able to be the only person whom his mother could communicate with and therefore had a very close relationship with her throughout his life. Although she could write to other people and communicate through her letters, Eliza was able to teach Alec finger alphabet, which he learned exclusively to communicate faster and better with Eliza (Gray, 8). This method of finger alphabet would prove to be a very effective knowledge for Alec later in his life when he became a renowned teacher for the deaf. Alec was also taught how to play the piano by Eliza who was a good pianist. She learned to hear the notes of the piano by attaching an ear tube connected to the sound board to her ear (Bruce, 22). His brilliant skill at piano, like his knowledge in finger alphabet, would eventually brighten his future by helping him meet Gardiner Hubbard at the Hubbard's tea party. Due to his closeness with his deaf mother, Charlotte Gray states, Alec was "untouched by the assumption, common at the time, that somehow deafness involved intellectual disability" (Gray, 8). His belief that deaf people can still learn and that their disabilities are not caused by their intellect is what shapes his curriculum as the teacher of deaf later on in his life. Ever since he was a child, Alec was very close with deaf people, and perhaps with deafness as well, mostly due to the influence Eliza had on him.

Like his relationship with his mother, Alec's relationship with his father was a challenge. Alec's father, Melville Bell, was a "Professor of Elocution," whose main achievement was his invention of "Visible Speech." Before the Visible Speech, Melville Bell, or "Professor" Bell as few called him, was known for being able to fix anyone's stammer and any speech impediment (Boettinger, 42). He was most known for being a "speech pathologist," someone who specialized in fixing people's lisp (Grosvenor and Wesson, 15). Melville was also a renowned researcher and a writer. In 1892, his *Standard*

Elocutionist ran 168 printings in England alone and about quarter of million copies were sold in the US (Grosvenor and Wesson, 16). Even though he gained fame from his research and textbooks on speech and phonetics, Melville's earnings were just sufficient enough to have his family of five live comfortably. He was never able to obtain great wealth like Alec did because his publication of Visible Speech was never really accepted by the world but he was still rich enough to be able to support his children's tuition at Edinburgh's Royal High School (Gray, 10). Visible Speech, Melville's pride and joy, was a system of symbols that depicted the movement of one's tongue, the breath, and the lips. Charlotte Gray calls it Melville Bell's "obsession with universal phonetic system" (Gray, 9). Nevertheless, he managed to come up with his chart completely on his own, looking at his own reflection in the mirror and writing down notes while uttering sounds and hisses. The outcome of 15 years of research, *Visible Speech: The Science of Universal Alphabetics*, was finally published in 1867 (Gray, 9). In it, Melville described his symbols from basic horseshoe that depicted tongue to vertical lines that depicted the breath in between sounds. He also created a new class of sounds (other than vowels and consonants) and called it "glides," claiming them as being halfway between vowels and consonants (Bruce, 40). Melville Bell's father proclaimed that his "invention will certainly be esteemed as one of the wonders of his wonderful age" (Bruce, 42). He also received praise from his colleague, Alexander Ellis, saying that his work was "a very ingenious and useful invention" and that it was "worth studying" (Bruce, 58). However, even though Melville claimed that a person who mastered his Visible Speech would be able to reproduce any sound exactly as it should sound, people thought of it as abstruse. Melville was certain that it would revolutionize the speech system around the world. However, its lack of success did not help Alec's relation with his father (Grosvenor and Wesson, 23). Melville's domineering manner and his constant urges to promote Visible Speech through Alec when he was in America teaching the deaf, exhausted Alec. Throughout Alec's life, he would be constantly bothered by impatient letters from his father asking about the reception that his Visible Speech was receiving in America.

This presented Alec with another problem to overcome, Visible Speech. Even though Alec had no interest in his father's Visible Speech, he mastered it when he was still in Edinburgh, only because of his strict father's demand (Gray, 13). However, Alec eventually overcame his problem with his father and Visible Speech. To fulfill his father's dream of seeing his work universalized (and also to stop his father from nagging him), Alec promoted Visible Speech during his lessons at the schools in which he taught deaf students. His lessons awed many skeptics, who saw visible progress. These deaf students, who have never heard how a certain word should sound, were able to pronounce that word perfectly after Alec's lesson (Bruce, 76). However, even after Alec's attempts to promote Visible Speech in America, most people still regarded sign languages and lip-reading as the method to teach the deaf.

Other than his problems with his parents, his siblings also caused problems in Alec's life. Shortly after moving to London, the Alec and his family were struck with terrible tragedies, the deaths of family members. When the Bells moved to London from Edinburgh, Alec's grandfather had died. Shortly after that, while Melville Bell was busy looking for people to sponsor his Visible Speech, Alec's younger brother, Edward Bell, who had poor health since birth, had little chance against the pollution of the London air (Gray, 16). When they moved to London, Edward, also known as Ted, began to show the early symptoms of tuberculosis. In the nineteenth-century, there was no cure for TB and the contagious disease affected many people living in polluted cities such as London. Surely enough, Ted died in 1867 at the young age of eighteen (Grosvenor and Wesson, 32). Ted's premature death affected Eliza the most and caused her to clutch onto her two living sons evermore. However, both Alec and Melly (Alec's older brother) was old enough to live on their own. Melly had married Carrie Ottoway and became a father of a son. However, the son, Edward, died of tuberculosis in 1868 before reaching his second birthday. Then, another devastating blow hit the Bells hard. The once-charming and hearty Melly quickly became pale and his moods dropped, alarming his close friends. The worried parents sent Alec to help out his older brother and he obeyed. Alec dropped all classes he was attending and suspended all his experiments and research to help his dying brother (Costain, 69). On May 28, 1870, Melly Bell, the first son of Melville Bell and an older brother of Alexander Bell, died of tuberculosis at the age of twenty-five just two years after the death of Ted. Alec's mother locked herself in her room and wept for days as black crepe draped the house. The deaths of so many family members caused the depressed parents to decide to move to Canada. They (except Eliza) overcame their grief and decided to start anew in Canada where the fresh, unpolluted air would surely do much good for the family. Alec was reluctant to follow his parents because he was yet to graduate from the University of London where he was pursuing a degree while studying physiology and anatomy. Not only that, but Alec was also still teaching Visible Speech at small, private school in Kensington for deaf children, as well as trying to court Marie Eccleston (Gray, 17). However, Alec realized that his health was the main concern for his parents and decided it would be best to leave England and start anew in Canada. The Bell's arrived in Quebec on August 1, 1870 (Costain, 71). Tutelo Heights would be the home of Alec's parents until their deaths.

After the tragic deaths death of Melly and Ted, Alec became the only surviving child of Melville and Eliza and becoming independent became a challenge. His health was still an issue. After Alec returned to London in early June, 1870, after having been taking care of Melly until his death, Alec's parents realized that he had grown unnaturally thin and pale, looking quite unhealthy (Costain, 70). The report from a specialist who examined him saying that Alec was dangerously ill made his parents desperate for their last remaining son. Melville Bell made a decision to move to Canada to keep Alec alive. However, even though the Bells moved to Canada in search of fresh air, Alec would still suffer from his poor health throughout his entire life. He was never able to completely cure his constant headaches, but he managed to control them mainly with the help of his mother and, eventually, his wife. Throughout Alec's life in America, Eliza would regularly write to him checking up on his health and desperately urging him to take it easy and rest. She constantly wrote to him to come back to Tutelo Heights, where the Bells lived in Canada, to rest and where Eliza would be able to keep a close eye on his diet and amount of rest he gets (Gray, 71). It was challenging for Alec to be independent from his parents because the death of Alec's siblings caused Melville and Eliza Bell to try to hold onto Alec evermore.

Alec's health was an issue throughout his entire life because of his one habit; He had a habit of overworking. In London, Alec was busy trying to receive a degree and also tutor deaf children at the same time. He overworked himself as he barely slept while trying to juggle everything that was going on in his life, such as his schooling, tutoring, promoting Visible Speech, and experimenting on his own (Bruce, 110). Once he moved to Boston from Tutelo Heights in April 1871, he immediately over-engaged himself with tutoring and experimenting. By the time Alec moved to Boston, he was trying to invent the first two-way telegraph that could send multiple telegraphs at the same time through the same wire. The competition was fierce. And with the likes of Thomas Edison and Elisha Gray all competing to develop the multi-telegraph, Alec had no choice but to overwork himself to experiment during the night because he tutored during the day (Grosvenor and Wesson, 42). When Alec was teaching George Sanders, a five-year-old deaf boy, George Sanders's grandmother invited Alec to stay at their house in Salem. Alec would then tutor his students in Boston all day, arrive at Salem, teach George Sanders, and then retire to his room to begin fiercely experimenting with telegraphs (Gray, 46). Such hectic lifestyle did not suit Alec very well because he often had severe headaches after many sleepless nights, which further worried his mother. Every year when Alec returned to Tutelo Heights, Eliza found her son thin and pale as ever and made feeding him her primary concern. Alec was only able to sustain his health (although barely at some points in his life) because his mother, and later his wife, took care of him. His overworking nature did not change even when Alec became old and rich because he would spend sleepless nights in his private mansion in Beinn Bhreagh, experimenting and trying to invent something new (Eber, 38). His spirit of an inventor never allowed him to rest comfortably, and it surely worried his mother and his wife greatly but it also allowed him to be successful.

His passion for teaching, as well as the challenges he faced while he was a teacher, did not help his health and his habit of overworking. For Alec, his career as a teacher was as important to him as his career as an inventor, and he struggled to find balance between the two. His teaching career started early when he was still in high school. Back when he was attending the Royal High School in Scotland, Alec was forced to attend the prestigious school by his father who thought his son needed a "solid foundation in Latin and Greek since so many scientific words are derived from those languages" and since he would need a "stronger grasp of some of the science," which he would later learn in University of London, to accomplish his experiments and research on reproducing human speech (Weaver, 23). However, bored with the seemingly-uselessness of his high school education, Alec was known to skip classes and go bird-watching and collecting plants, shells, small skeletons, and occasionally bird-eggs (Bruce 25). The Royal High School's lack of emphasis on science education sparked the creation of The Society for the Promotion of the Fine Arts among Boys. A group of Alec's friends met around outside of school to share acquired knowledge in scientific fields. Alec took the title of "professor of anatomy" and gave "lectures" and performed dissections. Hence, these were Alec's first lessons in his long teaching career (Gray, 11). Robert V. Bruce remarks that the society was the beginning of "Bell's dreams of scientific glory" (Bruce, 249). Later, at the age of 16, Alec (and his brother Melly) found a teaching job at a nearby Weston House Academy in Elgin, Scotland, in exchange for credit toward tuition for University (Weaver, 27). He taught music and elocution and in exchange received ten pounds, as well as further instructions on Latin and Greek (Gray, 13). By the time he was 18, Alec's family had moved to London where Alec took on another student, the family's Skye terrier, Trouve. Even though the dog lacked physical humanistic attributes to create human sounds, Alec taught his dog to "speak" by forming the correct shape with the dog's lips, tongues and jaws (Grosvenor and Wesson, 29). While the dog growled, as Alec trained him to, Alec would open and close the dog's mouth so that the dog's growling became "Ma ma ma ma." Placing his thumb under the dog's lower jaw, Alec then taught his dog to say "Ga ga ga ga." Many more "lessons" followed and soon he was able to teach his terrier how to say "How are you, Grandmama?" Although what Trouve really managed to say was, "Ow ah oo, gamama," the visitors who came to see the talking dog after they heard rumors about him didn't mind (Gray, 16). Other than his lessons with Trouve, Alec's teaching career continued, presenting more challenges. With the help of his father's contacts, Alec soon found another teaching job in Somersetshire College in Bath in England in 1866. He took French lessons while he taught evening classes (Bruce, 53). While he was attending the University of London, he taught his first deaf children at a private school in Kensington with his father's Visible Speech (Gray, 17). And with that, Alec's career as a teacher for deaf children had started. He taught deaf children by drawing a face (as well as the inside of a mouth) and erasing all parts except for lower lip, the point, front, and back of the tongue, and the glottis. The remainder of the drawing directly correlated with the symbols of the Visible Speech and taught the children the parts of their mouth that needed to be used for Visible Speech. This method of teaching deaf children about Visible Speech that he created proved to be extremely effective not only in Miss Hull's school in Kensington but also at the Boston School for deaf-mutes, and Gardiner Hubbard's Clarke School for the Deaf in Northampton (Bruce, 83). His passion for teaching never died down and until the day of his death, Alexander Graham Bell considered himself as a teacher of the deaf above all else.

Alec had to overcome more challenges while teaching in Boston. During that time, Alec's primary concern was inventing the multi-telegraph before the likes of Tomas Edison and Elisha Gray. His secondary concern, however, was as much problematic as, if not more than, his primary concern. He was broke. Until much later in his life when his telephone began to be commercialized, Alec always struggled to make a living even for himself. One of the main reasons why Alec had to keep teaching deaf children, even though he wanted to spend all his time experimenting with telegraph, was that he needed all the money he could get. He was a poor Scottish inventor who needed money to keep his research going. While tutoring deaf children and desperately looking for money, Alec found his patron. Gardiner Hubbard was a very rich Bostonian entrepreneur whose daughter, Mabel Hubbard, was a student of Alec. Alec had been teaching Mabel for quite a time when he met Gardiner Hubbard for the first time at the tea party at the Hubbard's massive house. At the time, Gardiner Hubbard was looking for an inventor to sponsor in order to compete with the telegraph giant, the Western Union Corporation. The Western Union Corporation, previously known as the Western Union Telegraph Company, had created a monopoly in the telegraph business. Since Gardiner Hubbard and his allies were trying to compete with the giant corporation, Hubbard needed a brilliant mind that could beat Thomas Edison, who had been chosen by the Western Union to invent, in creating the first multiple telegraph (Coe, 76). However, on the day of the tea party, Gardiner Hubbard had no idea that his daughter's tutor was experimenting in the midst of the night with telegraphs. Nor did Alec know that Gardiner Hubbard was looking for an inventor like himself and had the financial capacity that Alec desperately needed. The two men would meet soon to become partners and through Gardiner Hubbard, Alec was able to overcome his financial problem. Not only that, Alec also was able to marry Mabel Hubbard, his prodigious pupil and a daughter of his benefactor.

Marrying Mabel Hubbard was a challenge that Alec was not prepared for at first. Mabel came to Alec at first as a fifteen-year-old daughter of a rich Boston lawyer in 1872 (Grosvenor and Wesson, 48). She and Alec were ten years apart in age, and there were no signs of any romance between the young, rich, and carefree girl and busy, poor, and exhausted Scot at first. Gardiner Hubbard, Mabel's rich father, had seen Alec teach at the Clarke Institution for Deaf Mutes, where Alec spent few months teaching lip-reading and Visible. He then decided to hire this young Scottish teacher for his deaf daughter. Mabel was different from any other student that Alec had encountered and her personality soon captivated Alec. She had lost her hearing after suffering from Scarlet fever when she was five years old. However, she had a gifted mind and was brilliant at lip-reading. Not only her talent, but her high spirits and eagerness also allowed her to fly through Alec's lessons (Gray, 67). Alec was fascinated with her fast progress and surely enough, the relationship between Mabel Hubbard and Alec Bell began to develop as Mabel grew older. However, getting past the difference in their social classes proved to be quite a difficult task for Alec and this challenge forced him to spend many painful months waiting for the right time. Not only that, Alec was also very strongly opposed by the people around him, such as his parents.

Alec had hard time persuading his parents. His mother, Eliza, wrote worriedly, "if she [Mabel] is a congenital deaf mute, I should have great fears for your children." Author Charlotte Gray questions Eliza's intention for writing this peculiar letter. Gray writes, "Why did Eliza, who was deaf herself, react like this? In particular, why did she use the derogatory label 'deaf-mute'?" (Gray, 111). Even though Mabel Hubbard was not a congenital deaf, Alec had not told her that information. Since women who were congenitally deaf were likely to give birth to deaf children, she was worried for Alec's sake. Alec's relationship with his parents suffered a setback while he was trying to court Mabel, especially since his mother described Mabel using the derogatory term, "deaf-mute. Alec's father also disapproved.

> His father wasn't happy with Alec spending his time chasing a girl and did not respond to Alec's letters, angering Alec even more. Alec shared his anger towards his parents with Gertrude Hubbard, Mabel's mother. Gertrude Hubbard, who knew Alec was just an emotional man, persuaded him to write to his parents again even though he announced that he would not write to them again until they responded properly. He reluctantly obeyed and wrote, "Should this also be received with the same shameful neglect as my last I feel that there is danger of a complete

alienation of my affections from home (Gray, 112).

Such hostility between Alec and his parents endangered their relationship, but, after few exchanges of apologetic letters and the eventual acceptance of Mabel by Alec's parents, Alec was able to keep his relationships with his parents.

Persuading Mabel's parents proved to be a less stressful, yet still a daunting task for Alec. Persuading Mabel's mother was especially easy, since she already liked the young Scotsman, and his ability to play the piano so well. Because Gertrude was the first person to encourage Alec to propose to Mabel, Alec often sought guidance from her when trying to persuade other people, such as Gardiner Hubbard. Since Alec was young and very emotional, he proved to be surprisingly impulsive. He often barged into Mabel's house just to see her. However, when he couldn't tell Mabel his true feelings, even after many obsessive and impulsive visits to the Hubbard Estate, Alec sought guidance from Mabel's mother (Gray, 95). He wrote in one of his early letters, "I have discovered that my interest in my dear pupil…has ripened into a far deeper feeling…I have learned to love her" (Bruce, 151). Alec was very impatient when it came to waiting for Mabel. He halted his experiments and research, to the dismay of Gardiner Hubbard, who wanted him to finish inventing the multiple telegraph, to go after Mabel, who had traveled to her aunt's in Nantucket on July 1, 1875 (Gray, 102). He obsessively wrote to her and blurted out his feelings when it was inappropriate to do so (Bruce, 154). While he was chasing Mabel around in Nantucket and disregarding his experiments, Gardiner Hubbard expected him to settle down with his assistant, Tom Watson, and finish producing the multiple telegraph. However, Alec was too emotionally excited to settle down. Gardiner Hubbard was growing impatient with Alec by the day and announced that Alec would not have Mabel unless Alec started working on the multiple telegraph. He wrote to Alec, "I have been sorry to see how little interest you seem to take in telegraph matter" (Gray, 118). While Gardiner Hubbard and Alec were fiercely arguing, the whole problem was resolved by the bold decision of Mabel Hubbard. Mabel was a wonderful woman who was able to deal with his obsessive nature, and she already had feelings for her private tutor. So, two days after her eighteenth birthday, on November 27th, 1875, Mabel Gardiner Hubbard became engaged to Alexander Graham Bell, thus beginning a lifelong partnership and ending Alec's long struggle to marry Mabel (Bruce, 161). Alec was able to overcome their social differences as well as the oppositions of the people around him with unfaltering (and obsessive) love towards Mabel that eventually swayed not only Mabel, but also his parents and Mabel's parents as well.

Once Alec was able to calm his emotions and settle down as Gardiner Hubbard wanted him to, he needed to overcome his scientific challenges in making the multiple telegraph and the telephone. Until he was finally engaged to Mabel, Alec had yet to create the multiple telegraph that his patrons, Gardiner Hubbard and Thomas Sanders (the father of Alec's former student, George Sanders), were so desperately waiting for. Gardiner Hubbard urged Alec to focus on creating the multiple-telegraph before his competitors did, since Thomas Edison had been hired by the Western Union Telegraph Company to invent the multiple telegraph. However, Alec's mind was divided as he was unable to discard his idea of transmitting sound through wires (Gray, 92). He had the idea about the "speaking telegraph" ever since he conducted an experiment using tuning-forks back in Britain. In the winter of 1865, Alec found a way to determine the precise pitch of certain vowels. Because he had a very keen perception on sound, Alec was able to sound a certain tuning-fork and match that sound with a certain vowel that he spoke. Robert V. Bruce writes that "the tuning-fork experiment was his first step on the road to inventing the telephone" (Bruce, 46). His analysis on the compound pitches of human speech help shape the mouthpiece of a telephone. After his tuning-fork experiment, Alec wanted to create a "telegraph" that could transmit vibrations of sounds through wires instead of creating a telegraph that could send multiple telegraphs at once. Alec was born with an absolute-pitch, or perfect-pitch as it is more widely known (Gray, 80). This skill distinguished Alec from his competitors, such as Edison and Gray, when inventing the telephone because they did not understand the complexity of human sound and its vibration better than Alec did.

Alec had a tough time inventing the telephone, but the telephone was not his first scientific struggle. Alec's very first scientific challenge was when he was asked to create a machine for removing husks from grain for a local mill-owner (Gray, 11). The local mill-owner was a father of Alec's friend, Ben Herdman, and the boys worked hard to help Mr. Herdman. Alec created the machine with rotating paddles connected to the brushes inside the machine which would force the grains against the brushes, cleaning them of the husks (Bruce, 26). Another exposure to scientific experiment came when his father, after having seen Sir Charles Wheatstone succeed in making a machine pronounce human words, challenged his two sons, Melly and Alec, to create a "Speaking machine" (Grosvenor and Wesson, 17). While building this machine, Alec was exposed to Melville's anatomy books, and with his thorough knowledge of the phenomenon of human sound, he was able to channel his special knowledge and skills into creating his telephone. Alec and Melly divided up the work in that Alec was in charge of shaping the jaw, upper gum, hard palate, teeth, tongue, and lips out of rubber, wood, and wire. Melly, on the other hand, was in charge of creating a larynx of tin and rubber that would act to provide the machine with "breath" (Gray, 2). After the machine was put together, Alec manipulated the lips, palate, and tongue to produce a human-sounding gibberish. The boys decided to produce the most basic combination of sounds by opening and closing the mouth, producing the sound "ma ma ma" (Bruce, 37). Alec and Melly actually succeeded in making a machine that could "say" the words "mama" (Costain, 42). Alec later wrote, "The making if this talking-machine certainly marked an important point in my career" (Grosvenor and Wesson, 23). The speaking machine by Melly and Alec wasn't the first challenge that Alec faced in the world of inventing. Due to his upbringing and constant exposure to inventing, he was able to overcome his shortcomings of having no proficient knowledge in electrical science with his more than proficient knowledge in sound.

Even with his years of experience with scientific experiments, when Alec was trying to invent the telephone, he needed help. He had a very extraordinary assistant in the name of Thomas Watson. Alec and Watson's first encounter was at an electrical shop at which Watson was an apprentice. Alec was there because the workers had not followed Alec's directions when building parts of his harmonic telegraph apparatus (Boettinger, 60). Watson was a skillful mechanic working at the Charles Williams' electrical shop (Coe, 10). However, it was Watson who missed Alec's directions in making the device. Alec confronted Watson, and in doing so told him of Alec's plans for inventing the harmonic telegraph, which Watson decided to be part of (Gray, 83). Alec's investors, Mr. Sanders and Mr. Hubbard, have offered to pay for the salaries of Alec's assistants to help Alec reach his goal, so Thomas A. Watson became Alexander Bell's assistant in 1875 (Shulman, 71). Alec greatly appreciated Watson's craftsmanship. Watson's nimble and deft fingers helped with fine tuning the apparatus since Alec lacked such sensitivity (Grosvenor and Wesson, 52). He let Melly do all the fine tuning when they built the speaking machine in London. Watson, on the other hand, was absolutely fascinated about Alec's theories and eagerness, as well as his "punctilious courtesy to everyone" and his "clear, crisp articulation" (Gray, 85). Later, Watson became a full-time assistant to Alec in exchange for 10 percent interest in the telephone patent (Coe, 12). With Watson, Alec would complete his invention of the telephone and have the first telephone conversation with him.

Creating his long-thought-of invention, the telephone, was perhaps the most daunting challenge in Alec's life, mostly because it occupied majority of his life. Ever since he conducted the "pitch-fork" experiment and was exposed to the wonders of sound, Alec had been dreaming of sending sound through wires. When Alec was in London, he was living in the center of scientific conversations at the time. And the already-scientifically-excited Alec met the controversies and theories head on when he attended the University of London. Henry M. Boettinger states that, "No age could have furnished greater stimulus to the energetic and curious minds of people like the Bells" (Boettinger, 44). Just before he left for Canada, Alec was introduced to an experiment conducted by a German scientist Hermann von Helmholtz, in March, 1866. Helmholtz had conducted an experiment very similar to Alec's tuning-fork experiment to determine the musical note of the vowels. Alec's close friend, Alexander Ellis, wrote to him after Alec enthusiastically told him of his discovery on his tuning-fork experiment, "I find you are exactly repeating Helmholtz's experiments" (Bruce, 47). This excited Alec because at the age of 19, he had independently thought of the same idea as great scientist like Helmholtz. Helmholtz's device was an electric tuning-fork sounder that kept the tuning forks at constant vibration. Using electromagnets and coils, Helmholtz sent intermittent currents through to sound the forks (Shulman, 47). Alec was fascinated by this invention. However, Alec wrongfully thought that Helmholtz have successfully sent the synthetic vowels sounds, created by the tuning-fork sounder, from one point to another over an electric wire. Alec was mistaken because he wasn't able to completely understand Helmholtz's book, which was written in German (Gray, 43). However, Alec's misunderstanding on Helmholtz's achievement actually inspired him to invent the telephone later on in his life.

Alec had all the ideas of creating the telephone, but he had to come up with an actual device. In Alec's attic room at 5 Exeter Place in Boston, Alexander Graham Bell and Thomas Watson worked hard to create a device that could transmit sound through wire. In June, 1875, they succeeded in creating the first apparatus for telephone. It consisted of wooden frame and tightly stretched parchment drumhead for the membranes. However, the prototype was a disappointment because even though they were able to transmit sound through wire, they could not make out the words (Gray, 93). The first real transmission of sound through wire, and the first real success with the telephone, was with Alec's liquid transmitter. The device used dilute solution of sulfuric acid and it successfully transmitted the first words spoken through the telephone, "Mr. Watson, come here, I want to see you!" These memorable words, spoken by Alexander Graham Bell through his telephone to Thomas Watson, set off the two inventors into perfecting their magnificent device (Shulman, 14). Soon, Alec and Watson had the two-way conversation over the telephone, and on October 9, 1876, they succeeded in performing a two-way, long-distance telephone conversation (Bruce, 204). After many improvements throughout the years, Alec and Watson would perform the first transcontinental telephone call in January 25, 1915 from New York City to San Francisco (Gray, 400). Alec, with the help of Watson, was able to overcome the challenge of inventing the telephone and fulfill his dream of seeing his childhood idea becoming reality.

Having the working prototype completed, Alec was faced with an opportunity that he could not pass up in the early 1876, the World Exhibition. However, Alec was determined to stay at his school, where he was teaching deaf children, and give out the final exam, rather than attend the World Exhibition in Philadelphia. The prestigious exhibition was going to celebrate the hundredth anniversary of the American Revolution and Gardiner Hubbard was one of the three Bostonians in charge of organizing contributions from Massachusetts in the field of education and science (Gray, 130). Gardiner Hubbard was not going to miss this opportunity to tell the world of his inventor's new device, the telephone. By this time, Alec and his assistant, Thomas Watson, had successfully constructed a device that could transmit sound from the transmitter to the receiver through a one-way wire. However, Alec was reluctant to go show off his device in Philadelphia when he had commitments in Boston (Costain, 156). Expectedly, Gardiner Hubbard was furious about Alec's indifference to publicizing his invention but this was Alec's personality. Throughout his life, Alec never cared about publicizing his inventions like his rivals, like Thomas Edison, did. This obviously created many conflicts between Alec and his patron, Mr. Hubbard, who wanted to make profit from Alec's inventions by commercializing them, but Alec never had the mindset of creating an invention just to make money off of it. He invented for the sake of conducing scientific experiments and resolving his scientific inquiries. However, if it weren't for Gardiner Hubbard's threatening demand to attend the World Exhibition in Philadelphia, Alec would have not left his classes, and he might have never had a better chance to publicize his invention. Alec obeyed the command of his patron (mostly because Gardiner Hubbard told Mabel to tell Alec to attend) and attended the exhibition, achieving tremendous success and publicity for his "seemingly-magical" instrument that could speak on its own. Alec and his assistant, Willie Hubbard, demonstrated the telephone and attracted an eager crowd fascinated by the device (Weaver, 54). Although, people at the exhibition, which included Pedro II (or Dom Pedro) the emperor of Brazil, President Ulysses S. Grant, Dr. Joseph Henry, and other scientific celebrities, did not fully understand the capability and the potential of Alec's telephone (they saw it as a toy), it was still beneficial to Alec's publicity and Gardiner Hubbard's business interests (Costain, 161). Persuaded by Mabel and her father to publicize his invention, Alec was able to take another step towards his success in marketing the telephone.

With the success he achieved at the World Exhibit in Philadelphia in 1876, Alec had to patent his ideas before anyone stole them. Prior to meeting his patent lawyer, Alec, who could not afford a patent lawyer, relied on secrecy for protection in fear of his unpatented ideas being stolen by his competitors. Not only did he have a table made with a cover that could be securely locked, he also made most his own equipments because he could not trust the craftsmen. He even wound the coils of his electromagnets himself (Bruce, 94). Extremely fortunately, Alec was already acquainted with a patent lawyer. His patron, Gardiner Hubbard, was in fact a fully-proficient patent lawyer and he was more than willing to help his Scottish inventor patent the telephone (Grosvenor and Wesson, 49). Patenting his invention was easy because Gardiner Hubbard was an exceptional patent lawyer. Fortunately for Alec, Gardiner Hubbard applied for a patent on the "speaking telegraph" just two hours before Elisha Gray applied for his patent on the idea of the telephone on the morning of February 14, 1876 (Bruce, 167). This two-hour-advantage was extremely crucial, more crucial than Alec realized, because the U.S. Patent Office recognized Alec as the inventor of the telephone and not Elisha Gray. Had Gray applied for a patent before Gardiner Hubbard did, then Elisha Gray would have been regarded as the creator of the telephone. Author, Seth Shulman, wrote, "As I soon learned…the timing turned out to be a key to Bell's legal victory over Elisha Gray" (Shulman, 103). Once Gray applied for his patent, two hours later Gardiner Hubbard did, a caveat was filed that warned other inventors that Elisha Gray was working on telephony. However, unlike Alec, who had a working prototype, Gray had not succeeded in creating a device yet, thus not allowing him to apply for a full patent (Gray, 122). The U.S. Patent Office issued the United States Patent No. 174,465 to Alexander Graham Bell on March 7, 1876 for his "speaking telegraph" (Coe, 1). His first battle regarding the patent was over. He had triumphed.

Even though the U.S. Patent Office officially issued the patent on "telegraphy" to Alec, during the course of his life, Alec would be challenged by other inventors claiming that they invented the telephone before Alec did. These litigation battles, more than six hundred separate cases involving the telephone, took place in court rooms, where Alec was force to defend his title as the "inventor of telephone" against the impostors (Gray, 198). Western Union Corporation, for example, was selling Alec's patented telephones illegally while Alec was enjoying a long, relaxing family vacation in London. Seeing the Western Union outselling the Bell Telephone Company (Alec's company), Alec's two investors, Gardiner Hubbard and Thomas Sanders, hurriedly called Alec back to testify in court that he was *the* inventor of the telephone and file a suit in 1876 against Western Union for illegally selling the patented item (Coe, 79). The other court cases mostly involved inventors claiming that they came up with the idea of telephone before Alec did, but Alec never had any trouble disproving those hopeful inventors trying to discredit Alec. The list of hopefuls included, Elisha Gray and Amos E. Dolbear, who even after the court ruling, were convinced that they came up with the idea first, and Daniel Drawbaugh, a machinist from Pennsylvania who could not remember how he came up with the idea of the telephone but testified that he couldn't apply for a patent because he had no money (Gray, 198). Although many of court cases were ruled without the need for Alec to personally appear in court, there were two major cases that required his appearance. The first, which started in March 1883, involved Daniel Drawbaugh. A group of businessmen from Cincinnati and New York had created the People's Telephone Company by paying Drawbaugh $20,000 for his claim to have invented the telephone. The company sold pirated telephones and was sued for infringement by the Bell Company. After eight years of litigation, in 1891, Drawbaugh's claims were rejected and the Drawbaugh Case was over (Bruce, 275). The other case that required Alec's appearance involved Dr. James W. Rogers from Tennessee and much "political shenanigans," which made the case a "much murkier, more complicated one," according to Charlotte Gray (Gray, 200). Rogers, with his business partner, Casey Young, intended to stretch out the court case until Alec's patent expired because as long as the case was in court, any alleged infringers could continue their business. Their company, the Pan-Electric company was involved in the trial until Alexander Bell gave his fullest consecutive account of his telephonic work during the nine weeks in the spring and summer of 1892 when Alec was allowed to testify (Bruce, 277). Eventually, he emerged as the legal owner of the title, "inventor of telephone" and his patent No. 174,465 remained his, even after years of bitter legal battles (Cole, 186). It was mainly because Alec kept such organized notes on his ideas and inventions and these notes, such as the sixty volumes worth of "Laboratory Notes" in the Bell archive, were able to help him sustain his patent (Gray, 201). These litigation battles wore Alec out because he already disliked the business competition and did not liked to get involved. He also struggles to keep his name and his reputation as clean as possible through the court cases that were publicized. But with the help of his business partners, Alec was able to overcome any litigation challenges that came his way.

As Alec was enjoying his success of the Bell Telephone company, he was presented with a rather special challenge as a very special young girl named Helen Keller appeared in his life. A large part of Alec's later life involved this young girl as Alec spent much of time and effort to help her succeed. Helen Keller arrived at Alec's door with a knock in the early 1886. She was with her father, Captain Arthur H. Keller, a former Confederate officer (Gray, 266). They were from the small town of Tuscumbia, Alabama (Schuman, 77). Helen Keller, as a six-year-old girl who was both blind and deaf, was a wild, angry, and uneducated child. Since she could not speak, Helen often kicked, scratched, and screamed in order to communicate with her parents (Carson, 88). When Helen was nineteen months old, she suffered from high fever and her illness left her unable to hear or see (Lash, 43). The Keller family doctor told Helen's parents that she had an "acute congestion of the stomach and brain" (Keller, 26). However, after seeing Helen react to the vibrations of the watch he gave her, Alec concluded that Helen had no brain damage and recommended Captain Arthur Keller to see Michael Anagnos, the director of a school for the blind called the Perkins Institution in Boston (Schuman, 78). That particular recommendation changed Helen Keller's life, forever. In her book, *The Story of My Life*, Helen Keller wrote, "But I did not dream that that interview would be the door through which I should pass from darkness into light, from isolation to friendship, companionship, knowledge, love" (Keller, 16). Anagnos recommended a former pupil of the Perkins Institution called Annie Mansfield Sullivan (Gray, 269). She was a twenty-year-old who had spent four miserable and haunting years in a poorhouse in Tewksbury, Massachusetts, and suffered from trachoma that made her a near-blind (Bruce, 401). Miss Sullivan is often regarded as the "miracle worker" for her lifelong companionship with Helen Keller and Alec made it all happen. Alec not only found a teacher willing to teach Helen, but he also helped pay for Helen's education (Have, 109). With the help of Alec, Miss Sullivan was able to educate and transform Helen. Alec also helped her in a time of professional need. When Helen Keller gave a speech, Anne Sullivan always repeated what she said to the audience to make sure everyone understood. However, when Helen was scheduled to give a speech in New York at a meeting for the blind, Miss Sullivan was sick and could not perform her usual role. Helen sent a telegraph to Alec desperately asking for Alec to repeat her speech. Alec immediately stepped in and stood by her side while she gave the speech (Pasachoff, 102). His passion for education for the deaf allowed him to care for Helen until his death. In 1916, Alec stated that "Recognition of my work for and interest in the education of the deaf has always been more pleasing to me than even recognition of my work with the telephone" (Pasachoff, 103). He was very proud of his lifelong work with the education of deaf children, from England to the United States.

In his later years, the brilliant Scottish inventor, the inventor of the widely-used telephone, spent most of his time trying to invent something new for the sake of inventing since he did not have to worry about making money. Alec, very wealthy with all the money he made from the telephone, bought a huge estate called Beinn Bhreagh in Nova Scotia, Canada. Ever since he took a cruise tour of the place with his wife in 1885, Alec was captivated by the beauty of the region and bought pieces of the land over the course of seven years, from 1885 to 1892 (Gray, 246). When he finished buying pieces of the estate, he built a magnificent mansion for his family at the furthest point of the estate overlooking the Bras d'Or Lake called Red Head (Grosvenor and Wesson, 145). During his 37 years in Beinn Bhreagh until his death, Alec's new challenge was creating a new invention. However, this did not come easily for the aged inventor. His attempts gave birth to abstract ideas, such as attempting to transfer brain-waves using wires connected to his head. This "scientific" experiment in 1888 consisted of wrapping a coiled wire around his own head, then wrapping the same wire around his assistant's head. Alec believed that he could transmit ideas, or thoughts, without speaking, through the wire into his assistant's brain. After the failed experiment, Alec wrote in his notes, "All that was shared was a headache" (Gray, 254). He did, however, succeeded in few experiments. By the time Alec bought Beinn Bhreagh, he was very interested in heredity and attempted experiments to breed ewes with extra nipples. Since the word "genetic" would not even be coined until 1905, Alec was "groping in the dark as he tried to understand the role played by genetic heritage," according to Charlotte Gray (Gray, 297). He spent months numbering, weighing, and measuring every sheep. In 1904, Alec reported to the National Academy of Sciences of his success at breeding ewes with at least four milk-producing nipples (Bruce, 416). Other successful attempts at inventing included the invention of the tetrahedral kites, which later paved the way for Alec to invent the flying machine, and the invention of the HD jet boats.

Just as many inventors were working on the multiple telegraph and telephone during the 1870s, many people were working on flying machines in the 1890s, including Alec

(Schuman, 84). Alec heard the news that the Wright brothers from Kitty Hawk, North Carolina, had succeeded in the world's first flight in a heavier-than-air machine on December 17, 1903 (Pasachoff, 105). Alec, approaching his sixtieth birthday, longed to mark his name in the world of aviation, so formed the Aerial Experiment Association (AEA) in October 1, 1907, to "successfully demonstrate manned motorized flight" (Haven, 99). Mabel Bell not only funded the AEA, with $20,000 she made by selling her property in Washington, but also sought out young men to help her husband in his quest for aviation and found Frederick (Casey) W. Baldwin, Douglas McCurdy, Lieutenant Thomas E. Selfridge, a West Point graduate who Alec arranged with President Theodore Roosevelt to be an official observer for the U.S. Army, and Glenn H. Curtiss, an engine expert (Pasachoff, 113). The AEA's first invention was a giant tetrahedral kite named *Cygnet*, consisting of 3,400 tetrahedral cells, and its flight was on Friday, December 6, 1907 (Gray, 369). Even though Alec wanted to use his patented tetrahedral shape in making the planes, the other men in the AEA, who were all educated engineers, persuaded Alec to build biplanes, like the one made by the Wright brother (Schuman, 96). After *Cygnet*, all three inventions by the AEA were biplanes. The *Red Wing* was built by Selfridge on March 9, 1908, the *White Wing* was built by Baldwin on May 18, 1908, the *June Bug* was Curtiss's invention on July 4, 1908, and AEA's fourth and last biplane, the *Silver Dart*, was built on February 23, 1909 by McCurdy (Bruce, 451). The *June Bug* won the Scientific American trophy for being the first heavier-than-air airplane to fly more than a kilometer in the fall of 1908 (Gray, 373). The *Silver Dart* set ten speed, endurance, and altitude records during the early 1909 (Haven, 99). Alec and his men certainly left their marks in the world of flying with their success in aviation.

When his prized AEA approached its end on March 13, 1909, Alec kept himself busy with hydrofoils. His began to think about airplanes taking off from water with his first sketch of hydrofoil in 1906 (Pasachoff, 118). The first of Alec's four hydrofoil machines, the HD-1, "HD" standing for hydrodrome, roared through the water with its fifty-horsepower engine in 1911 (Gray, 404). All four of Alec's HD's looked like stubby planes floating in water because of their wings. Hydrofoils are underwater wings that allow the ship to be lifted higher than water and "fly" through water (Haven, 103). Over the next few years, Alec built three more hydrofoils with little success until the World War I broke out in Europe in 1914. He continued after the war broke out, but as the war edged toward North America, he felt that as a citizen of a neutral country, he should not work on an invention that could have military uses (Bruce, 469). However, his last HD, the HD-4, with its 350-horsepower engine, was capable of speeds of 71 miles an hour (Haven, 103), and roared across Bras d'Or, the lake next to Beinn Bhreagh, in November 11, 1919 (Gray, 410).

In the last year of his life, Alec lamented, "I cannot hope to work out half the problems in which I am interested" (Pasachoff, 118). His other inventions never managed to outshine Alec's world-famous telephone, but they still prove that even in the waning years of his life, Alec was a brilliant and eager inventor who was never discouraged when it came to experimenting and whose spirit of an inventor was never extinguished until his death on August 2, 1922 (Gray, 425). He was never satisfied being just an inventor. He was always a teacher first. Alec once told Helen Keller by spelling the words on her palm, "One would think I had never done anything worthwhile but the telephone. That is because it is a money-making invention. It is a pity so many people make money the criterion of success. I wish my experiences had resulted in enabling the deaf to speak with less difficulty. That would have made me truly happy" (Eber, 71). His success as a teacher of the deaf was more important to him than his fame and monetary success. He was happy to invent for the sake of inventing and gaining knowledge, and this mindset set him apart from his competitors, like Thomas Edison, who cared for monetary success, and allowed him to become the acclaimed inventor renowned for his invention of the telephone that revolutionized the way people all over the world communicated with each other.

At 4:30 PM on January 25, 1915, in the midst of a large crowd gathered around at the New York City headquarter of AT&T, an old man, in a frock coat and white waistcoat, sat down at the end of a long table. Having thrown aside the script that the event organizer had prepared for the special occasion, the old man, the founding father of telephony, picked up the phone knowing exactly what he was going to say and to whom he was speaking to. Alexander Graham Bell spoke on the first transcontinental telephone call: "Hoy! Hoy! Mr. Watson, are you there? Do you hear me?" Alec's words traveled from New York City to San Francisco. Thomas Watson replied at the end of the line that stretched over 3,000 miles: "Yes, Mr. Bell, I hear you perfectly. Do you hear me well?" (Gray, 400). After a few minutes of chatting, Alec repeated the words he had spoken 39 years ago, on the historic day when Alec and Watson made the breakthrough with the telephone. As he once did on March 10, 1876, Alexander Graham Bell spoke to his faithful assistant:

"Mr. Watson, Come here, I want to see you.

Bibliography

Benson, Sonia and Jennifer York Stock. *Development of the Industrial U.S., Reference Library, Edition 1.* Detroit: U·X·L, 2005.

Boettinger, H. *The Telephone Book.* Croton-on-Hudson: Riverwood Publishers, 1977.

Bruce, Robert. *Bell: Alexander Graham Bell and the Conquest of Solitude.* Boston: Little, Brown, 1973.

Carson, Mary. *Sterling Biographies: Alexander Graham Bell: Giving Voice to the World.* New York: Sterling, 2007.

Coe, Lewis. *The Telephone and Its Several Inventors.* Jefferson: McFarland & Co, 1995.

Costain, Thomas. *The Chord of Steel.* Garden City: Doubleday, 2000.

Crompton, Samuel. *Alexander Graham Bell and the Telephone.* City: Chelsea House Publications, 2008.

Davidson, Margaret and Stephen Marchesi. *The Story of Alexander Graham Bell: Inventor of the Telephone.* Milwaukee: Gareth Stevens Publishing, 1997.

Eber, Dorothy. *Genius at Work.* New York: Viking Press, 1982.

Gray, Charlotte. *Reluctant Genius.* City: Arcade Publishing, 2006.

Grosvenor, Edwin and Morgan Wesson. *Alexander Graham Bell.* New York: Harry Abrams, 1997.

Haven, Kendall. *Alexander Graham Bell*. New York: Franklin Watts, 2003.

Keller, Helen and James Berger. *The Story of My Life: the Restored Edition*. New York: Modern Library, 2004.

Kids, for, Time, of, Editors and John Micklos. *Alexander Graham Bell*. London: HarperCollins, 2006.

Lash, Joseph. *Helen and Teacher*. Reading: Addison-Wesley Pub, 1997.

Pasachoff, Naomi. Alexander Graham *Bell*. Oxford Oxfordshire: Oxford University Press, 1996.

Pelta, Kathy. *Alexander Graham Bell*. Englewood Cliffs: Silver Burdett Press, 1989.

Schuman, Michael. *Alexander Graham Bell*. Springfield: Enslow, 1999.

Shulman, Seth. *The Telephone Gambit.* New York: W. W. Norton & Co, 2008.

"Steve Jobs and Apple, Inc."

Amy Jeon
The Academy of Holy Angels

Steve Jobs created Apple, Mac, iPod, iTouch, iTunes, and more. He was the brain and innovation behind all of his creations. If you do not know Apple in the twenty-first century, you are not from the twenty-first century. Apple started the connecting line between personal computers and media, like songs and videos. The solid fact that all these great inventions that changed our world came from only one person is probably very hard to comprehend. Just looking at all the Apple products and how great they are, we must think the person who made all these must also be great. However, the standard of greatness in gadgets and greatness in people are very different. Great gadgets are called great when they can do many things that are useful in a short amount of time. However, a great person is commonly referred to as a hero who is benevolent to others. Steve Jobs is a hero for sure (at least for millions of Apple worshippers/consumers), but he is not at all benevolent or nice to other people. Rather, he is elitist, perfectionist, bossy, picky and demanding. He only works and even talks with the A-Team, as Jobs would call them, and is the pickiest person on earth. He is very hard to approach and hard to satisfy. Anything that comes out of him must come out as perfect. He sure can yell and denounce anyone who does not satisfy him. However, Steve Jobs, elitist and the most obnoxious person to be around, is still the king of modern technology world. Apple sells billions of their products every month. Why is that? Why does the world love his inventions and his creative mind behind them? Why does everyone go crazy whenever Apple comes out with a new invention? Why does everyone scream and applaud whenever Jobs goes on the stage to give a presentation about his "babies", iPod, Mac books, and more? Why am I begging my mom for a new Mac book even when I have a perfectly usable PC? The answer for all these questions is simple; Jobs thinks better and farther than any of us, and he can make others want what he wants.

But one thing is very clear. Steve is the hardest person to satisfy; he is pure perfectionist. He only pursues perfection in everything. His perfection made him to think differently even when Apple was making their first retail store appearance. Until the 1990s, most of the stores sold their products from a huge department store where all the companies' products were mixed together. In order to buy new clothes or computers, customers had to come to the huge department store and see all the choices from different companies and choose from there. However, in that way, small, unknown companies like Apple could not be recognized among other huge companies like Microsoft or Dell. After Gap revolutionized retail by dropping other brands and concentrating on its own line of clothing and its revenues took off like a rocket, many clothing stores followed Gap and started to have their own retail stores with only their clothes. However this was not common in technology world even until the late 1980s. This was mostly because computers were not commonly used that time and consumers did not demand any particular company; they just simply did not care about what computer company they buy.

However, Steve Jobs once again thought differently; he wanted his Apple computers, his babies, to look perfect in a perfect place with perfect employees. He did not want his babies to be pushed away by other companies in a department store. So he hired Mickey Drexler, one of the best retail store designers, and worked with him to make the first and the best retail store for computers. He did not care how much it would cost him to be perfect because all he wanted was perfection. Jobs knew he had to get a location in a populated place such as trendy shopping districts where people go to look for new goods for their lives. So people could come to buy clothes or something like that and somehow, intentionally or unintentionally, go in to Apple's store to look at its goods. Now, Jobs was perfectly aware that getting a store in a high-end malls and trendy shopping districts was very competitive and expensive. However, he was also aware that he needed the store in these places for Apple. Because even if the customers left without finding or buying any product, they would not care if they waste twenty footsteps to Apple store in the mall but they would care if they waste twenty minutes of car ride to Apple store in a low rent strip malls on the edge of the town. So Steve Jobs chose the expensive trendy shopping districts, not to waste money but to gain more customers and more money in the end.

Surprisingly, all of Steve's longing for the best things brings the best results. For example, the retail store for the Apple which everyone thought was a risky action for an unknown company like Apple, at least at that time, to take turned out to be the best success. Apple opened its first retail store, placed in a trendy shopping mall and far away from a big department store where all the computers from different companies were stacked up on each other, on May 19, 2001, in Glendale, California. Since then, its chain of more than two hundred stores has become the hottest thing in retail. It is the fastest growing in retail history. Its retail stores reached $1 billion in annual sales in just three years, breaking the record previously held by The Gap (Kahney 203). By spring 2006, its stores were making $1 billion every quarter (Kahney 203). This is way over the amount Steve Jobs had to pay for his first store. Everyone was sure it was a risky step and that it would never succeed but just after five years, it is the best retail store in the world. So, where exactly did this success come from? Some probably came from Mickey Drexler's amazing retail techniques and some probably came from the location of the first store. However, the most part of its success came from Job's great desire for the best.

Jobs once had an interview with Fortune magazine and talked about his success in Apple's retail stores. "So we did a few things. No.1, I started asking who was the best retail executive at the time. Everybody said (Millard) Mickey Drexler, who was running the Gap," (Kahney, p.115) Jobs told this to Fortune magazine very proudly. In fact, he does have a right to be proud because he took a risky step that no one could take because they were afraid it would not work. He chose the best people to make the best things and the best result came out. This is how Job's brain works and his theory about only having the A players is the most obvious theory. Only best people can do best things simply because they are the best.

The same result came out from Apple's ad as well. The commercial must have been very expensive since Lee Clow, the best commercial designer, made it but it left the most famous and the everlasting title "Think Different" for Apple which brought many new customers in to recognizing Apple and its products. In 1984, Apple ad, "Think Different", was on introducing the Macintosh during the third quarter of the Super Bowl. "It turned out to be fortuitous: the ad garnered more attention and more press than the game itself. Although it was shown only twice (during the Super Bowl and earlier, on an obscure TV station in the middle of the night to make it eligible for advertising awards), the ad was rebroadcast in countless news reports and on *Entertainment Tonight*. Apple estimated that more than forty three million people saw the ad, which was worth millions of dollars in free advertising, according to an estimate by then-CEO John Sculley." (p.128 from Inside Steve's Brain) Even now, people still think of the "think different" ad when they think of Apple.

The Apple's ad was very typical of Jobs; it was bold and brash. Unlike other commercials of its time that only presented their products, Apple's ad was more like a mini-movie with characters, a narrative and high production values and won people's attention. Jobs once again proved to be a complete elitist and won by being smart enough to team up with Lee Clow and Jay Chiat, the best commercial designers at the time. The ad went on to win at least thirty five awards for Chiat/Day, including the Grand Prix at Cannes, and generated millions of dollars (Khaney 128). Because of this ad, many ads that time which only described the products straightforwardly tried to be like the Apple's ad which had the story line to capture their customers while looking at it. Even now, many ads that we see in televisions have a story line which leads to the products and explains why they are good. This explains how Apple's ad was not only an interesting commercial for that time period; it ultimately became the cultural realm. It not only changed the commercial business, but it changed what people expect from a commercial.

Steve Jobs sure is an elitist who only works with the best people in the field. He was like that from the beginning. "Jobs is an elitist who believes that a small A team is far more effective than armies of engineers and designers. Jobs has always sought out the highest quality in people, products, and advertising" (Kahney, p. 107)). Even when Apple was a no name company, he still pursued the best employees to work for him. When looking for a great designer for his first Macintosh, he set up a designing competition so that he could hire one of the best designers. He did the same when making Apple's first advertising commercial. He worked with TBWA/Chiat/Day which is considered one of the most creative advertising companies in the world. Steve Jobs only desires and looks for elitists to work for him. He truly believes a small group of A team is so much better than a huge group of B team or C team. This is why he likes to keep his company small and only with the best people. Of course, there are other huge groups of engineers and manufactures who do work in Apple, but they are not as important as the small A group. They do not know anything about their products and their system until they are open to the public because Jobs likes to keep everything inside his A team. "I always considered part of my job was to keep the quality level of people in the organizations I work with very high," said Steve Jobs. (P.108 from Inside Steve's Brain)

In Apple, the employees are always on their toes thinking who is going to be fired today by Jobs. Their jobs are very insecure. In the company, there is a word that everyone knows and yet wants to avoid very badly; the word is getting "steved." Getting "steved" is basically getting fired by Steve Jobs with often bunch of harsh words that could hurt one's feelings very badly. Jobs is very good at determining whether a person is a bozo or an A team player. However, when he decides whether a person is a bozo or an A team, he either fires the person or hires the person. There once was a rumor around the company that going into a same elevator with Steve Jobs is the stupidest thing a man can ever do because Steve is probably the likeliest person to be able to manage firing a person and cutting off one's income line with only one or two minutes in a compact place like an elevator. If Jobs doesn't like the person, then he is immediately out. He has no pity or sympathy for anyone if he can make the quality of his work place higher. So, one can wonder why on earth anyone would ever want to work for Steve Jobs.

There are two reasons why people want to work for Apple. First, with A team members around, the environment's quality is very high. Thus Apple's working atmosphere challenges people to be better. This is what Steve Jobs wanted in his company; he wanted his employees to be challenged and also be able to challenge him. Steve Jobs determines whether a person is a bozo or elite by seeing how a person reacts when he is placed on a spotlight. He sees whether a person can still stand up for his belief even when he is questioned by many people. He puts people on their toes to see if they really care about their belief and trust that it is the truth. "Unless you have a lot of passion about this, you're not going to survive; you're going to give it up. So you've got to have an idea or a problem or a wrong that you want to right that you're passionate about; otherwise you're not going to have the perseverance to stick it through. I think that's half the battle right there." (Kahney, p. 113)This is how Jobs sees potential in people and it is also the whole purpose of Apple. He only takes and leads those ones who can persevere and hold on to their passion even though the wider world's reaction might be doubtful. Jobs believes one can change the world only with these kinds of people and with this highly challenging atmosphere.

Second, Steve Jobs discovers the A players. "We've made the leap from an idea centered business to a people-centered business. Instead of developing ideas, we develop people. Instead of investing in ideas, we invest in people." (Kahney, p.113) This quote is by Randy S. Nelson, the dean of Pixar University. Pixar, a company that Steve Jobs bought and ran as a CEO after he was forced to resign from Apple, uses the same method of "only A players" just like Apple. Companies that are run by Jobs have a unique similarity. They do not like to get bigger as the company gets bigger and like to discover A player qualified characteristics in people. Jobs is very good at discovering A players. Many geniuses do not realize that they are geniuses until someone tells them; Steve is that "someone". Outsiders may think working with Jobs would be like working in hell but those who are considered as A players by Jobs and who have worked with him for a while think differently. They actually thank him for discovering their talent and giving them enough room to express their talents. This is where Steve is right about keeping his company packed with only A players. Many critics of Apple may cut down his characteristics but at least it helps his company to grow and to be the best. Best people can make best things. Steve is not surprised by Apple's amazing products because he knows the whole purpose to get the best players is to win the game.

However, Steve is not extremely nice to the A players, either. He can still yell and be obnoxious even to those who he considers to be an A player, if he felt it to be necessary. However Steve can still be charming as he wishes to get an A player on his team. One of the A players that he had a hard time to bring in was Horn, a programmer who created the Mac's Finder— the heart of the Mac's operating system. Horn did not initially work at Apple; he had already taken a job with another company, VTI, which promised him a $15,000 signing bonus which was a large sum of money at the time. Horn recalled:

On Friday evening, I got a phone call. "Bruce, it's Steve. What do you think about Apple?" It was Steve Jobs."Well, Steve, Apple's cool, but I accepted a job at VTI."

"You did what? Forget that, you get down here tomorrow morning, we have a lot more things to show you. Be at Apple at 9 a.m." Steve was adamant. I thought I'd go down, go through the motions, and then tell him that I'd made up my mind and was going to VTI.

Steve switched on the Reality Distortion Field fullforce. I met with seemingly everyone on the Mac team, from Andy to Rod Holt to Jerry Manock to the other software engineers, and back to Steve. Two full days of demos, drawings of the various designs, marketing presentations—I was overwhelmed.

146

On Monday I called Doug Fairbairn at VTI and told him I had changed my mind. (Kahney, p.116)

Steve Jobs can be very charming and nice if he wanted to. He showed Horn what it is like to work at Apple and how much room Apple can provide for his imaginations and his visions to flourish. Many A players who work for Steve say that even if they had another chance to choose whatever company they would like to go, they would once again choose Apple and Steve Jobs. Now, these are people who are fully aware how mean and harsh Jobs can be. However, they also know that Jobs creates a space for them to discover their inner talents and how their inner talents were originally discovered by Steve Jobs. This is why people prefer Steve and follow Steve.

Jobs can be very obnoxious but very charming when he wants to be. This is another great characteristic he has. He can persuade people easily with this characteristic. Jobs is a person who goes on a walk to a park with another business man and has a contract signed. He is also a person who goes up on a stage with few slides behind him and absolutely seduces customers to buy his products. However, he can also say "no" and other few harsh words to things he does not like. By being charming, he gets his contracts signed and his products sold. And by saying "no", he saved his failing company.

After Steve resigned from his position in 1985, John Sculley became the next CEO of Apple. Many things went wrong after Sculley came in control. First Apple started to make "clone" companies such as Motorola and Umax. By making these "clone" companies, Apple allowed these companies to use Macintosh operating system. Apple believed that these companies would benefit Mac market but it eventually failed. Other companies started to take sales away from Apple and in 1996 Apple lost sixty nine million dollars and laid off one thousand three hundred staff. (Kahney, p.16-17) The company was now in bankruptcy for six months; they needed a hero to magically save their company. In 1997, Steve Jobs finally came to rescue his beloved company, Apple. He made few changes when he came back. He knew these "clone" markets provided customers with cheaper prices and no one actually bought

Apple's computers from Apple. So he first cut down all the "clone" companies. This was the first thing he did when he came back also because sharing his beloved Apple just did not make any sense to Steve even if the strategy did work. He knew in order for him to have an absolute control of Apple, it had to start alone. He also tried to simplify Apple's products until only the necessary things were the only left products. He thought Apple could not afford or manage all the different products. He thought it was better for Apple to focus on few products and make them far more special and superior than any other computers. So he gathered his A team players and got a whiteboard and drew few lines to make two by two grid and wrote "consumer" and "professional". Then he wrote "portable" and "desktop" in the other grid. So now Apple only focused on four machines unlike other companies who are launching so many versions of each product. Apple had two notebooks and two desktops, aimed at either consumers or professional users. This simplified strategy was so much clearer and easier. Now, workers could focus on few things and that concentration brought perfection in products.

Apple stresses a lot on simplicity of its products. Steve thinks that simplicity and cutting down all the choices except the only necessary ones is a way to truly think of customer's points of view. Engineers are often pressured to add more features to new versions of their products which are marketed as "new and improved." Most companies think more features mean better value and media emphasizes the new features. However Apple tries to resist this the most because having more choices ultimately comes down to confusion. Steve not only simplified the product pipeline of the Apple, he also practiced his idea of simplicity in many other Apple's products like iPod and Macs. For example, Macs are often criticized because of its weak power engine and limited gigabytes. However this is also a way to prevent Macs from constantly getting viruses and getting lagged. PC users have to suffer from the viruses and a lot of lagging processes but Mac users hardly ever experience these things. Apple tries to simplify everything. One can listen to a song and change to another song in just a few clicks on iPods. Jobs also made the complexity of computers disappear from his Macintosh. He did not put any expansion slots, so it would have very limited memory. Everyone argued that a computer that does not have an expansion slot would be doomed because without it, it would be so under-powered and would not be easily upgraded. However Jobs thought farther than that; no expansion slots can also mean a simplified machine.

One of the features that many great companies have is having a focus group. A focus group is for researching what customers want so that the company could be more customers centric. This may sound like an obvious tactic because companies want to make things that customers want. However Steve thinks in a way that was never thought by any other CEOs. He says that customers do not know what they want unless they are shown what they want. Henry Ford, one of Steve's role model, once said "If I had asked my customers what they wanted, they'd have said a faster horse." (Fortune Magazine, p.112) Steve goes with this model and not with having a focus group to research about customers' wants because customers are totally blinded to what they want unless someone makes a device to tell them that the device was what they wanted. This was proved to be the right way to tackle customers' wants by iPod, iPhone, and Macbooks. Steve didn't create a snazzy, portable, easy to use music player like iPod because he was told by his customers that it was what they wanted. He somehow knew better and faster than anybody else and had a vision of a functional and pretty music player. He somehow knew that his customers would love it. This is the same with iPhone and Macbooks. He had a vision of a familiar, "friendly-looking" device for his customers and showed it to his customers and successfully made them wanting it. Now why is it that only Steve gets these visions among all the other talented CEOs or designers? And why is it that customers only like the things Steve somehow knew they would like? When we look at the bottom of Apple's devices and compare them to other companies' devices, we can see why. Apple's devices are truly customer centric while other companies' devices pretend to be customer centric by having all these fancy focus groups. When other companies launch their new product, they report that the device is truly customer centric and that it has everything customers want. However, who are these customers to be truly called as a regular customer like you and me? A regular customer should not know anything about the gadget because we are not trained to know. We should just decide whether we like it or not when the gadget comes out as a finished product. So having a focus group doesn't necessarily means the gadget completely tackled what the customers want. As Steve said, customers are there to be astonished by the finished products, not to choose what they want or tell the companies how to make the product; that is what CEOs do.

Other companies not only pretend to be customer centric, they also fake it. When companies start launching their new product, they usually have a video or a presentation to show how "easy" their product is. However, it only seems easy because the one who is showing how to use the product is probably an engineer or a CEO who should know how to use the product. It is a totally different story when it's the customers' turn to use the product. It is just like looking at your teacher do an example problem for you and thinking you fully understand the concept. However, when you come home and do the problems by yourself, it is so hard that it almost feels like a totally different question even though the question is exactly the same. Other companies do not care about how the customers would feel when they are at home with their new product; they only care about how cool and amazing their product will look on a commercial or a video so that they can get as many customers as possible to buy their new product.

Apple does not pretend or fake customer centric and this is why Steve's visions successfully target what customers want. Steve tries to think in a customer's point of view and looks at a gadget or thinks of a gadget as if he were totally new to technology. He seeks for the simplest device with a sleek design and he literally makes the gadget so easy to use that the customers will not even realize how much efforts went into making it so easy. And Apple said that was their goal. Their goal was to simplify all the possible choices for the customers so that they won't have to think and choose as much. Apple wants their products to be part of their customers' every day life. They want it to be so usual for the customers. And how can a complicating, multi-tasking gadget be a part of a customer's every day life? Apple wanted computers to be used not only by hobbyists or geeks, like few decades ago, but by just an ordinary person. Jobs wanted to make a computer that could be entertaining and enriching people's lives. That soon became the roots and the core of Apple's sincere customer centric.

Steve also involves a lot in designs. He just does not approve or disapprove the designs at the conference tables; he actually works as part of the designing team and comes up with ideas. Many people compliment and admire Apple's designs. They are so simple yet fashionable. Computers weren't supposed to look this good; they were supposed to look confusing and ugly for the geeks. However Apple's designs totally changed how people want their computers. During 1980s and 1990s, computers did not have any space for pretty designs. Computer companies had to put so many things such as software programs and chips; they thought making computers "pretty" and "friendly looking" would be impossible. So the computers that time were all boxy and bulky. Computers had a bulky edges and "non friendly looking" boxes attached to the monitor which were the expansion slots. So the computers were only accessible and usable by the hobbyists and geeks who knew everything about computers just like those workers who actually make the computers. However Jobs did not like this idea. He wanted to make his computers look "friendly" and approachable even to any common people who absolutely know nothing about computers. In order to make these computers, he needed pretty and round designs and just plain, simple computers that could be easily used by normal people. So he hired Hartmut Esslinger, a German industrial designer in his mid-thirties and the winner for the design competition for the first Macintosh set up by Steve Jobs, came up with a design that no computers had during that time. His design, "Snow White", made Steve's Macintosh look totally different from other bulky, ugly computers. It had round edges and vertical and horizontal shapes which made it look smaller than other computers. Esslinger also used these stripes as ventilation slits to prevent objects like paperclips being poked inside the Macintosh. Also he used the highest quality manufacturing processes, known as zero-draft. Even though it is more expensive than other processes, zero-draft molding made Apple's cases small and precise which Jobs like the best about the Macintosh. Apple's Snow white design won many design awards and the design eventually became so widely adopted by other computer companies that it became the industrial standard for computer case design.

Apple is no longer recognized as just a company that produces computers and technologies. It is more like a part of the culture of this generation. Whatever Steve Jobs comes up with becomes a hit. All the Apple's products are always on the must have lists. Apple's computers are not just for professional computer users or just for teenagers. They are used by so many different groups of people. They all have different wants and needs and they all expect different things and they use a computer for different reasons. However Apple's products just seem to be the only computer that can satisfy all of them. Steve does not question what people want, he rather shows what they want and discover their wants before anyone else does. He may be obnoxious and selfish and may have some anger management issues but he still gives people what they want. He also loves his job and has a great passion for it. Steve once talked about Bob Dylan, one of his mentors, and said that one of the things he admired about Bob Dylan was his refusal to stand still. Many successful artists at some point in their careers they keep doing what made them successful in the first place, but they don't evolve. If they keep on risking failure, they are still artists. Steve innovates and moves forward despite the possible failures. He was forced to resign from his position as CEO in Apple, and even when he came back to Apple he had few failures such as Mac G4 cube which was overly centered on design and not function and lost few billions of dollars. Recently, he had to go through cancer. However Steve still stood up for his passion and beliefs and kept searching for perfection. Many might be able to find few faults in him but he is still on the top of this generation and he is not afraid to move forward. He sure can be called as a hero and not that many can oppose that.

Bibliography

Kahney Leander. *Inside Steve's Brian*. New York: Portfolio, c 2008

Fry, S. (2010, April 12). "iPad Man". *Time*. 40-43.

Grossman, L. (2010, April 12). "Apple's Next Big Thing." *Time*. 36-40.

Lashinsky, A. (2009, November 23). "CEO of the Decade", "The Decade of Steve." *Fortune*. 89-100.

Copeland, M. (2009, November 23). "The Apple Ecosystem", "Character Builders", "Music to Their Ears", "Apple Finds Its Calling", "His Legacy." *Fortune*. 102-114.

Okrent, D. (2009, November 23). "The Books of Jobs", "All About Steve." *Fortune.* 117-126

"Ray Bradbury"

James Kim
Paramus High School

Ray Bradbury is still considered one of the greatest writers of the 20th century. With his charismatic voice that was heard in his writing style, he was able to publish hundreds of books that changed many people's perspective on life. (http://www.spaceagecity.com/bradbury/bio.htm) He was a very versatile writer, writing science fiction novels such as *The Martian Chronicles* to also writing futuristic, dystopian novels like *Farenheight 451*. Besides writing, Bradbury also directed movies, help build buildings, and taught many lectures. Bradbury believed that he needed to help the society as much as possible, and this was a big motivation in many of his decisions.

Ray Douglas Bradbury was born on August 22, 1920 in Waukegan, Illinois. He was raised by his parents, Leonard Spaulding Bradbury and Esther Marie Moberg who were recent Swedish immigrants. (http://www.gradesaver.com/author/ray-bradbury/) His father was a lineman for an electric company, so Bradbury and his family lived in a non-luxurious lifestyle which actually helped Ray later along in the future.

His family's name was known to be very wild and crazy in their childhood. He was related to the Spaulding family, the family that created the sports equipment, and also related to Douglas Spalding, the American Shakespeare scholar. Bradbury would often talk about them in his books such as in *Dandelion Wire*, he has a crazy character named Douglas Spaulding, but he would never say it was them directly.

However, Ray never lived up to his family name. In fact, he was the complete opposite. Ray grew up as a very shy kid

154

who didn't have a lot of friends. Ray eventually learned how to associate well with others, but it took a while.

Bradbury's family couldn't provide a lot for Bradbury, but the one thing they could provide was love. Not only his immediate family, but also his extended family such as the Spauldings would always support Ray and give him a lot of attention. This provided a great foundation for his career and his books.

Ray had many interests as a kid, but he had one main interest. Many might think it would be writing for sure, but surprisingly, it wasn't. It was magic. The first time he went to a carnival, in 1932, he met a magician named Mr. Electrico. He put a sword on his nose and yelled "Live forever!", which made his hair stand straight up. Ray was so fascinated by this, that he immediately went home and studied magic. It is surprising that Bradbury became a writer because for the majority of his childhood, he focused on magic. If Ray had not found writing as his true love in his childhood, he would have surely been a magician.

After Bradbury's encounter with the magician, he began to write daily, whether it was about magic or his favorite book he recently read. Although he lacked in financial resources as a kid, one thing Ray could always count on was the library. Bradbury would spend countless days and nights, even as a child, looking up books that he would enjoy and reading all of them, thus making him an anti-social kid. The majority of his childhood was actually in the Carnegie Library, in Waukegan, Illinois. Bradbury would enter the library knowing that he is surrounded by unlimited books that he could read at any time, and that pleased him.

Perhaps Bradbury's biggest influence though, was his Aunt Neva, who was a costume designer and a dressmaker (http://www.notablebiographies.com/Be-Br/Bradbury-Ray.html). She encouraged Bradbury to pursue a career of acting or writing. Aunt Neva would often tell Bradbury to use his imagination, and that is probably why Bradbury is the great writer he is right now.

From ages 6 to 13, Bradbury had constantly moved around. He moved back and forth from Waukegan, Illinois to Tuscan, Arizona, once from 1926-1927, and again from 1932-

1933. This was because his father was seeking a better job to support his family. However, he could never find the right job, so they eventually moved to Los Angeles permanently, which Ray and his family fell in love with.

What Bradbury loved the most about Los Angeles was all the action that goes around and all the celebrities that lived there. In fact, Ray would often rollerblade through Hollywood just to see if he could spot any celebrities to get their autographs or even just talk to them. This made Bradbury a more social person who finally had the courage to talk to more people. This also helped Ray gain wisdom from experienced, well-known people who know what it takes to go on the big stage. Some of the celebrities he met eventually became mentors to him like special effects expert, Ray Harryhausen and radio star, George Burn. Even more so, George Burn hired Ray for his first job as a writer for the *Burns and Allen Show*.

When Bradbury entered high school at Los Angeles High School, he pursued the career of acting. As inspired by his Aunt Neva to act, Bradbury was always curious about being an actor, and he had a great opportunity to learn about it because he lived in Los Angeles. He was surrounded by friends and family who also pursued acting so Bradbury could not help at least try to get into acting. He was inspired by all the celebrities he met and he wanted as much, if not more fame than the ones he looked up to. He joined the drama team to help him become a better actor, but two teachers helped him realize his true talent: writing.

Bradbury's English teachers, Snow Housch and Jeannet Johnson, helped him further develop his writing skills once they realized his tremendous writing skills. They specifically taught him how to write short stories and poems, and certain styles on how to write; even now, his work is evident and reflecting upon what he learned almost 70 years ago. These two teachers helped Ray change his course from wanting to become an actor to wanting to become an author. This is why he joined many new groups such as Los Angeles Science Fiction League and the Poetry Club to help him be a better writer.

After high school, Bradbury wanted to go to the military, but he was immediately rejected because of his poor eyesight.

Bradbury decided to just spend his time making money selling newspapers while getting his education from libraries. His family didn't have much money and it was the Great Depression at the time so Ray thought it was best to not attend college. Ray was quoted saying, "Libraries raised me. I don't believe in colleges and universities. I believe in libraries because most students don't have any money. When I graduated from high school, it was during the Depression and we had no money. I couldn't go to college, so I went to the library three days a week for 10 years." Although his job pretty much took up his entire day, he still went to the library during the night to read and write. And although Ray never went to any colleges or got any sort of proper education after high school, he still ended up to be one of the smartest and most successful kids to graduate from his high school.

Ray's first published work was called "Hollerbochen's Dilemma," in 1938 which was a short story. However, it was in a magazine called *Imagination!* which wasn't mainstream and a still amateur magazine. In 1939, he started writing for his own fan magazine called *Future Fantasia*, where he wrote most of the magazine himself and wrote all four short stories that were ever written on the magazine. He finally found a book where he could write in when he found "Super Science Stories". This book was a paid publication; therefore, it was the first official writing piece written by Bradbury.

Obviously, Bradbury didn't immediately have success in the literary field, but he kept striving for great things. While Bradbury was just getting in the writing business, he looked up to many experienced writers for guidance and help. Henry Kuttner and Henry Hasse were one of many authors Bradbury looked up to. Not only did he look at their work to improve his own writing, but they helped Ray get to the next step from an amateur writer to a published, sophisticated writer.

Finally, Ray realized that he wanted to write in books instead of newspapers, so he finally quit writing in newspapers to pursue his full time job as an author. Ray wrote a short story called "The Lake" in 1942, and that is the point in his writing career where he found out the writing style he wants to write in. He continued to write short stories and in 1945, he wrote "The

Big Black and White Game", which received the honor of one of America's best short stories. This was when Bradbury was noticed by Americans in his skill to write.

In 1946, Bradbury met his future wife, Maggie McClure. Maggie was a graduate of George Washington High School and UCLA. She came out of college and worked at a book shop as a clerk. Ray was at the book shop at the time, and they began to talk. They got married a year later in the Church of the Good Shepard. Ironically, Ray's best man was Ray Harryhaesun, one of his most important mentors when Ray was still a kid. Ray and Maggie had four daughters: Susan, Ramona, Bettina, and Alexandra.

The year Bradbury got married, he released his first collection of short stories called, "The Dark Carnival". This was his first solo book that was released by an official publishing company. The publishing company's name was Arkham's House, but they were only a small press in Sauk City, Wisconsin.

Ray Bradbury finally had the book that made him one of the most famous authors in America when he wrote the novel, The Martians Chronicles. Bradbury was very lucky when he gave the book to one of the most respected critics in the United States, Christopher Isherwood. Once Isherwood read the book, he could only marvel at the great writing piece. Isherwood praised it, saying, "... the sheer lift and power of a truly original imagination exhilarates... His is a very great and unusual talent." However, it was not well liked by everyone, including another well respected critic, Damon Knight, who said, "Although [Bradbury] has a large following among science fiction readers, there is at least an equally large contingent of people who cannot stomach his work at all ... His imagination is mediocre; he borrows nearly all his backgrounds and props, and distorts them badly; wherever he is required to invent anything -- a planet, a Martian, a machine -- the image is flat and unconvincing."

This was a science fiction novel, and this gave Bradbury a good reputation for his writing in science fiction. The book was based off a man who was trying to colonize Mars. This leads to an unprecedented reaction from the colonists in Mars and worsens the war with Earth. Another novel that became very popular, like The Martians Chronicles was the futuristic novel <u>Farenheight 451</u>. This book was about a possible futuristic scenario in the United States where the government burns all books to avoid the citizens from getting wrong thoughts and ideas. These two books have made Bradbury one of the most famous writers of the 20th century, and he became a household name throughout the United States.

Bradbury has won multiple awards during his time as an author for his short stories and his novels. He won awards such as the O. Henry memorial Award, the Benjamin Franklin Award, the Aviation Space Writer's Association Award, the Grand Master Award, The World Fantasy Award, and the Best Space Article in an American Magazine (http://www.spaceagecity. com/bradbury/bio.htm).

Although Bradbury has had a passionate love for books, he had an equal or if not larger affection for movies and visual arts. This led to his helping out in several movie productions including *Moby Dick* and *A Beast from 1000 Fathoms*. There was also many attempts to turn some of his books turned into TV shows including *The Twilight Zone* and *The Halloween Tree*. Bradbury was very pleased with these adaptions to TV shows, but he was very disappointed at the attempt to turn *Martian Chronicles* into a TV show.

As Ray began to produce a lot less literary works, he began to do other things. For example, he would introduce ideas to various projects such as *Spaceship Earth* and *Orbitron* in Disneyland. He also wrote the script for the United States Pavillion. In addition to being an "idea civic", he continued to give lectures and give lessons to the younger generation about broad topics such as writing techniques as well as storytelling.

Ray Bradbury, who is currently 90 years old, is still strong and healthy. He is still lecturing and teaching at various colleges, and at an age where most other people would be completely retired, Bradbury is still willing to share his wisdom to many others. He currently lives in Los Angeles, and in 2003, his wife, Maggie, unfortunately passed away. He has 8 grandkids and 4 cats which he spends most of his time with.

Ray Bradbury will ultimately go down as one of the greatest writers of all time. His versatility of writing with science fiction to fantasy, his ability to mesmerize his readers with his books, and his will to give back society will always be remembered. Bradbury always believed that he should give as much back to society as possible, and Bradbury has sure done that.

"Henry Ford"

Billy Kim
Clarkstown North High School

Henry Ford is one of the most influential Americans of our time. He was the creator and founder of what is now known today as the Ford Car Company. His achievements in life revolutionized how much the people of the present have access to a different, better, and faster means of transportation other than walking. He is the reason behind why we are able to produce faster goods and provide consumers with more products. His inventions are considered to be one of the foundations of today's economy. Throughout his life he had an aptitude for mechanics which helped him achieve all the things he had done and accomplished in his lifetime. His ideas and attitude as both an entrepreneur and as a businessman had all contributed in the Ford Company being one of the top automobile sellers in the world even to this day. Henry's life revolved around his mechanical genius and thinking. His compassion and devotion to mechanics granted him the title of being one of the most influential, and economical titans of all time.

Henry Ford's childhood was that of one expected of children of his time and age. He attended the public schools nearby his house. His years in school proved to be troublesome for his teachers because of a habit of having to pull and execute constant pranks. He had an interest in mechanics so he would carry around nuts, bolts, and machinery parts. Due to his interests aptitude in mechanics he was able to make and create machines that won him a title of being the top notch prankster by his friends and teachers. Although he would occasionally be criticized for his pranks by his parents, he would continue to show interest in mechanics. He was influenced the most by his mother, who taught him to work with both a happy attitude and to complete all his work. Henry once recalled, "My mother taught me to work"[1].As he worked on the farm and his interests in mechanics grew, he began to dislike the work of the farm and continued his pranks regardless. Even during class time he would sit at his desk and hide behind a textbook while he tinkered with his friend's watches, taking them apart and putting them back together. Henry once talked of how students with inappropriate behavior would be "placed directly under the teachers eye"[2], but he was rarely and almost never caught. Henry was able to reach all of his great achievements through his ideal way of thinking in mechanics as he had demonstrated in his childhood.

During his childhood he found a lifelong friend by the name of Edsel Ruddiman, who was a neighborhood boy, at a school called "Scotch Settlement School". He was inseparable from him and they spent almost their entire childhood with each other doing everything they could with each other which included a four mile walk to their church. Even though they weren't all that religious, they went together to spend more time together. Henry would always say, "Your best friend is one who brings out the best in you"[3], and he would mention his old friend Edsel and how he was able to become the person he was able to become with the help of his friend. As he grew, his childhood flew by as he spent his boyhood with his family and lifelong friend. In 1886, fed up with his son's (or what he thought was) pointless tinkering and contraptions, Henry's father made one last attempt in order to get Henry to quit his dreams of being an engineer and to become a farmer like he himself. Although Henry's father clearly saw how successful Henry had been with the farm machines he decided to make one last effort to anchor Henry down. Henry's father tried to make a deal that if he were to quit being machinist he would grant his son property of eighty

---

[1] Watts, Steven. *The People's Tycoon*. first ed. New York: Alfred A. Knopf, 2005. Print.

[2] Ibid

[3] Ford, Henry. "Henry Ford > Quotes." *Good Reads*. Web. 4 Sept. 2010.
<http://www.goodreads.com/author/quotes/203714.Henry_Ford>.

acres of land with a small house and abundant tree growth. Henry took the deal only to test his own mechanical expertise. Henry believed that "Whether you think you can, or think you can't, either way you'll be right"[4], with this quote he believed that only you can know your own expectations and limits. Through testing himself, he attempted to find his limits and meet his expectations. After attaining the land from his father he set up a lumbering (wood cutting) company and invented a new contraption, made out of a circular saw and portable steam engine. With it, his lumbering company prospered and soon started providing wood and lumber for his neighbors, shipyards, factories, and shops. As years passed he met and married Clara Jane Bryant, who was another reason why he had agreed to the deal made with his father. After his marriage, he led a life with a single foot on the agricultural past and the other foot on the industrial future. By this time he began to think about "horseless carriages" and was given an opportunity when he was hired to fix an Otto engine from England. He became obsessed with the gasoline engine and soon afterwards he began projects in order to build a better engine that was not only functional but lightweight unlike a steam engine. Henry would work day and night by himself in order to invent such an engine. Henry had once said that "Quality means doing it right when no one is looking"[5], Henry meant this to say to the people of America that another secret to success is having competence and patience to not just look good but be good, too. From there on his childhood ended and he passed into his manhood.

Henry ford's life as a machinist was very interesting and filled with small adventures, hours of tinkering, and countless days of thinking about machines and devices. Due to his mechanist thinking he always thought to seek easier ways to work on the farm. "I never had any particular love for the farm—it was the mother on the farm I loved." This quote was said by Henry whenever he was asked why he did not do the everyday

---

[4] Ford, Henry. "Henry Ford Quotes and Quotations." *Famous Quotes and Authors*. N.p., n.d. Web. 4 Sept. 2010. <http://www.famousquotesandauthors.com/authors/henry_ford_quotes.html>.
[5] Ibid

farm work like a normal farm boy. He would try to think of shortcuts to lighten the chores around his household. Henry felt that it was unnecessary to waste energy when he could simply find a faster easier and more efficient way to work while getting the job done.

Due to this way of thinking he was always scolded and called "lazy" or "rebellious". Henry had commented on this subject saying "Exercise is bunk, if your healthy you need it, when your sick you don't do it"[6], which means that Henry thinks that it is unnecessary to waste energy when he could execute the same action with the same or better results. He would have some success in trying to lift some of the burdens of farm work, but all in all, his attempts were quite futile. His mother had gained a habit where she would always tell someone to never give their possessions such as watches, wind up toys, and other tinkers because he would always just take them apart. Henry's mother would simply tell anyone who offered up there watches, "Don't let him have it, he'll only take it apart."[7] Henry's, as a child, fascination in mechanics gave him a hobby which soon turned into an obsession, repairing watches. A man by the name of Adolph Culling first took the back of a silver watch and showed Henry how each part worked and what they did. After he was shown the parts and functions of each of the parts Henry started tinkering with his classmates' watches.

He also gained a reputation along with his obsession as a skilled repairman. He spent countless hours visiting stores of other towns trying to buy and trade parts for his other mechanical devices. He made tweezers out of his mother's corset stays and a screwdriver out of a nail by grinding small indents into the point. He soon showed interest in larger and more complicated devices such as engines. His love for machines and tinkering gave him not only motivation and energy but patience and diligence. As soon as he turned his attention to engines his obsession was also averted to engines. From here on is when he began to start his dreams of having every average American own an automobile. Henry once said that "To see a thing clearly in

---

[6]Ford, Henry. "Ford, Henry Quotes." *Quotations Book.* N.p., n.d. Web. 5 Sept. 2010. <http://quotationsbook.com/author/2560/>.
[7] Ibid

the mind makes it begin to take form."[8] And with this quote he pictured in his mind an America filled with automobiles from the rich to every average man of America. With this new goal in mind Henry, instead of visiting towns for watch stores he went to every store that sounded anything similar to engine works. His new obsession with the engine wasn't with just the general body of it but the efficiency. He was crazed about how to make the car run faster, longer and smoother(less friction) for less amount of energy. Henry not only became crazed about the car's efficiency but also the people to whom they were selling to. Henry had said that "A business absolutely devoted to service will have only one worry about profits. They will be embarrassingly large,"[9] and with this quote Henry captured hearts of Americans only to further his position in power. His way of thinking, which is to try and get as much production as he could from the amount of energy used, made him the leader in devising projects but soon afterwards stepped aside as others   began to implement them. Henry's life was progressing forward when all of a sudden his mother, pregnant with her 7th child, died when the birth of the seventh went terribly wrong and both the mother and newly born child died. Henry's life went up side down and the sudden event was especially bad due to the fact that none of it was to be expected. He was devastated inside his heart and to have seen his beloved mother and newborn sibling pass away left emotional scars, which he carried for years and years. Henry had mentioned, "I thought a great wrong had been done to me when my mother was taken."[10] The death of his mother also started a tense relationship with his father.

Henry somehow blamed his father to be the cause of his beloved mother's death. Henry was known to have been closer to his mother much more than he was to his father. It was said, "He respected his father but would always turn to his mother for love and understanding."[11] The passing of his mother caused many

---

[8] Ford, Henry. "Henry Ford Quotes." *Brainy Quote*. N.p., n.d. Web. 5 Sept.   2010. <http://www.brainyquote.com/quotes/authors/h/henry_ford_2.html>.
[9] Ibid
[10] Ibid
[11] Ibid

problems to occur in his family as the oldest son entered his young adult hood with a chest filled with deep sorrow and pain. His father was sought by the oldest child as a dignified, stubborn, but kindly authority figure. The growing tension between Henry and his father also showed a broader and more historical dimension. Henry's relentlessness at the constraints of country life clashed with his father's values and experiences, and this lent additional force to their argument about Henry's career prospects and his future. Skipping ahead to Henry's life as a man, Henry found his wife at a dance in the Martindale House in Greenfield. He had been introduced to a pretty local girl by the name of Clara Jane Bryant by one of his cousins. He was stunned by her and was quite pleased. Henry and Clara courted and were engaged to each other on April 19, 1886. Due to Henry's lack of money they could not have a quick marriage. So when he was offered the Moir place by his father, mentioned in paragraph one, he saw a way to earn a respectable amount of money. After he worked for two hard years of work and saving he married Clara on April 11, 1888. Although they moved into Henry's old bachelor house they began to construct a new home. Henry constructs what is known today as the square house over the year of 1889. The new abode was a cottage with one and a half story floors; it was built with lumber from his farm and featured a wraparound porch, dormer windows, and gingerbread columns and balustrades. . They moved into the new cottage in June 1889.The next stage in his life was in 1896, Ford and Alex Dow was present at a convention in Manhattan Beach, New York. Thomas Edison was an honored and special guest at the evening's banquet. Alex Dow happened to point out Henry to Edison, telling him, "There's a young fellow who has made a gas car."[12] Edison asked young Henry Ford a host of questions and when the interview was over, Edison emphasized his satisfaction by banging his fist down on the table. Edison said loudly, "Young man, that's the thing! You have it! Your car is self-contained and carries its own power plant."[13] Years later, Ford, reflecting on their first meeting, said in a newspaper interview,

---

[12] Ibid
[13] Ibid

> That bang on the table was worth worlds to me. No man up to then had given me any encouragement. I had hoped that I was headed right. Sometimes I knew that I was, sometimes I only wondered, but here, all at once and out of a clear sky, the greatest inventive genius in the world had given me complete approval. The man who knew most about electricity in the world had said that for the purpose, my gas motor was better than any electric motor could be.[14]

Ford never forgot those words of encouragement. After that initial meeting, Ford was always very close to Edison. When Ford became a wealthy industrialist, he cooperated with Edison in technical and scientific projects. He convinced Edison to devote significant research to finding a substitute for rubber. Together with John Burroughs, naturalist Luther Burbank, Harvey Firestone and occasionally, President Harding, Ford and Edison participated in a series of camping trips. A major source of fun for Ford and Edison was building dams on small streams and examining old mills for a calculation of the power output. From here on his life as a businessman began.

Ford's legacy began when he became an engineer in 1891. He was an engineer with the Edison Illuminating Company in Detroit; the Edison Illuminating Company built electrical generating stations. This event signified a conscious decision on Ford's part to dedicate his life to industrial pursuits. His promotion to Chief Engineer in 1893 gave him enough time and money to devote attention to his personal experiments on internal combustion engines. His salary was increased to 125 dollars a month allowing him efficient money for his interests. In 1896 he built his first self-propelling vehicle called the "Gasoline Buggy", or the Quadricycle. Although making his first vehicle was important it was very limited in terms of speed and functions. The Quadricycle could have been roughly described

---

[14] Ibid

as a box with 4 heavy bicycle wheels attached to it, with a steering wheel similar to steering a tiller on a boat, and it only had 2 different types of speed it could have gone forward, and could not go backwards or go in reverse. Although this vehicle was not the first self-propelling vehicle built, Henry was still a major contributor to America's becoming a nation of motorists.

Henry then built 2 race cars named the "999" and the "Arrow". He hired a professional bicyclist and race car driver to race his new cars for him. After doing so Ford drove the "999" and the "Arrow" setting a new land speed record, which was over 91 miles per hour. Henry seeing his new cars as a success, he and 11 other investors tried to create a new company. After two unsuccessful attempts to establish a company to manufacture automobiles, the Ford Motor Company was incorporated in 1903 with Henry Ford as vice-president and chief engineer. Henry was a person who thought, "Failure is only an opportunity to start over again, only this time more intelligently." [15] Henry had invested twenty eight thousand dollars in the Ford company when it was made. The infant company produced only a few cars a day at the Ford factory on Mack Avenue in Detroit. Groups of two or three men worked on each car from components made to order by other companies. Henry Ford realized his dream of producing an automobile that was reasonably priced, reliable, and efficient with the introduction of the Model T in 1908. Henry had once said amusingly, "You can have the Model T in any color, as long as its black."[16] This vehicle initiated a new era in personal transportation. It was easy to operate, maintain, and handle on rough roads, immediately becoming a huge success.

By 1918, half of all cars in America were Model Ts. To meet the growing demand for the Model T, the company opened a large factory at Highland Park, Michigan, in 1910. Here, Henry Ford combined precision manufacturing, standardized and interchangeable parts, a division of labor, and, in 1913, a continuous moving assembly line. Workers remained in place, adding one component to each automobile as it moved past them on the line. Delivery of parts by conveyor belt to the workers

---

[15] Brinkley, Douglas G. *Wheels for the World: Henry Ford, His Company, and a Century of Progress* (2003).
[16] Ibid

was carefully timed to keep the assembly line moving smoothly and efficiently. The introduction of the moving assembly line revolutionized automobile production by significantly reducing assembly time per vehicle, thus lowering costs. Henry thought that "Before anything else, getting ready is the secret to success."[17] And this quote was very meaningful when he built the assembly line because the purpose of the assembly line was to speed up production by not just making the job easier but also having the workers ready to quickly attack or add their assigned part to the preassembled cars. Ford's production of Model Ts made his company the largest automobile manufacturer in the world.

The company began construction of the world's largest industrial complex along the banks of the Rouge River in Dearborn, Michigan, during the late 1910s and early 1920s. The massive Rouge Plant included all the elements needed for automobile production: a steel mill, glass factory, and automobile assembly line. Iron ore and coal were brought in on Great Lakes steamers and by railroad, and were used to produce both iron and steel. Rolling mills, forges, and assembly shops transformed the steel into springs, axles, and car bodies. Foundries converted iron into engine blocks and cylinder heads that were assembled with other components into engines. By September 1927, all steps in the manufacturing process from refining raw materials to final assembly of the automobile took place at the vast Rouge Plant, characterizing Henry Ford's idea of mass production. As he achieved his goal of mass production he soon began to reset his old goal of allowing every average American to own a car. Once he made a method of manufacturing that allowed him to earn more profits, he did not keep or pocket his earning but rather kept decreasing the prices of his cars. Soon afterwards, Ford was able to achieve his final goal by selling more cars and making the automobile a luxurious item for the average. Henry's goal was considered honorable and humble. Henry had commented in passing, "A business that makes nothing but money is a poor one."[18] Having achieved all

---

[17] Ibid

[18] Collier, Peter, and David Horowitz. *The Fords: An American Epic.* San Francisco: Summit, 2001 .

his life goals, Henry lived a full and satisfying life when he passed away at the age of 83 in April 7, 1947, four years after the death of his one and only son Edsel.

Henry had lived many different lives, as some people would say. He had a personal life, that of one of a dreamer, and the one as an emperor. Henry Ford and his inventions and models made him a titan of his time. In the 1920's Ford became one of Will Rogers'(a famous actor / American cowboy / comedian / humorist / humorist / social commentator / vaudeville) performer favorite topics. In addresses, articles, and radio commentaries, the popular humorist frequently joked about the industrial's (Henry) traits and influence in modern America. Ford "changed the habits of more people than Caesar, Mussolini, Charlie Chaplin, Clara Bow, Amos 'n' Andy, and Bernard Shaw,"[19] Rogers claimed once. He made fun of the model T saying that in Ford's world, a man's castle is his sedan. Rogers jokes reached its peak at "The Grand Champion," a 1929 essay that was on the American Magazine (a magazine company).Rogers focused on champions, a category he defined as being the best at any one thing, whether it was Bobby Jones and golf, Houdini at magic, or Al Smith as a second Columbus, Rogers nominated Henry Ford as the champ, who he said is someone who had influenced the world, our plain old friend Mr. Henry Ford. This choice set off a landslide of Rogers one-liners. Ford, "along with Brigham Young, is the originator of mass production."[20] Thanks to Roger and several other factors, Henry reached the peak of his reputation and influence.

The basis of his popularity remained from the Model T, which his companies' factories continued to produce by the millions throughout the decade. In addition, Ford's activities as an industrial reformer and former political candidate, along with his image as a folk hero and success icon, made him perhaps the most esteemed private citizen in the United States. His thoughts on every conceivable topic provided grist for the journalists' mill on almost a daily basis, and his comments were a sure fire attraction for readers throughout the country. Stories about him

---

[19] Ibid
[20] Ibid

and stories by himself appeared regularly in nearly every major magazine and newspaper in the United States. At the very moment of his triumph several deeply seated problems produced a wave of uneasiness. Amid the chorus of praise for his unexpected accomplishments, a few nasty comments and rumors could be heard. A small group of critics questioned Fords treatment of labor and his reputation as a reformer. As this critism took notice suspicion rose that Henry's reputation as an innotative industrialist rested on a unstable needle point. Whenever Henry was faced with such accusations he would say clever phrases like "Don't find fault, find a remedy"[21] and would always remain somehow optimistic. In 1923 the sales of the Model T began to decline in the face of growing competition. The General Motors Corporation developed a modern marketing and organizational plan in the 1920's that offered buyers and consumers a variety of price ranges. The corporation made Chevrolets, Pontiacs, Oldsmobiles, Buicks, Cadillacs and etc. while saying the quote "a car for every purse and purpose"[22] as their slogan. The motors corporation also developed better tires, brakes, and gears. Such competitors caused an internal division in the Ford Company, including his own son, pressured Henry to accept that the Model T was now obsolete and to make a new Model.

In addition, an economic recession early in the decade inspired a reorganization of the system by which the company distributed cars to its dealers, a move that caused bitter and a long lasting resentment. Meanwhile, an ambitious Ford proposal to gain the waterpower of the southeastern U.S. aroused growing opposition that eventually scuttled the project. This array of difficulties worked steadily to undermine Ford's public standing. The Ford Motor Company showed extreme signs of strain at the moment of its greatest triumph. External criticism of its emperor, Henry, was mounting while internal problems in his company were festering. Before long, the tension reached a critical point. Ford had controlled at least 40 percent of the American

---

[21] Ibid

[22] Kent, Zachary. *The Story of Henry Ford and the Automobile.* Chicago: Children's Press, 1990.

automobiles and that figure generally held steady throughout the first half of the 1920's. The booming market in the U.S. was increased by the internationization of the Ford product. Sales of Ford vehicles outside the U.S. climbed steadily after WW I, from fifty thousand in 1919 to ninety one thousand in 1925. Even more important was that the model of mass production, high wages, low prices, and widespread consumption, or Fordismus, had become very popular in Europe by the mid 1920's. In Germany their translation of "My Life and Work" sold rapidly, and at least a dozen books on Ford and his industrial innovations appeared. The most striking instance of Fordismus was in Russia. At the outset of the decade, the Soviet Government ordered a shipment of Fordson tractors to help control the crop failure and famine that was devastating the economy. Over the next few years, the Fordson tractors were sold by the thousands and the Russian peasants came to worship the tractor as a magical machine. Henry's "Fordizatsia" was a system that could bring inexpensive, durable goods to the masses, something the Russians saw Henry as a revolutionary figure for. Henry's reign as the emperor consisted of his company going back and forth with competitors and achieving further and further influence over the world.

In conclusion, Henry Ford who had an aptitude even as a child for mechanics had a vision of allowing the average American own a single car. He was a titan with a dream, a dream to let every average American own a single automobile. He achieved his goal by sacrificing useless human emotions such as greed and hate and made America into a nation of true motorists. He influenced the world with his unique way of thinking and inventions, making today's life as an American more luxurious and peaceful. He made today's world a better place by inventing the assembly line allowing faster production of goods and increasing the economy significantly. Henry Ford was one of the most influential men of America.

Bibliography

Allan Nevins and Frank E. Hill, *Ford*, 3 vols., 1954–62.

Barbara S. Kraft, *The Peace Ship: Henry Ford's Pacifist Adventure in the First World War*, 1978.

Brinkley, Douglas G. *Wheels for the World: Henry Ford, His Company, and a Century of Progress* (2003).

Brough, James. *The Ford Dynasty: An American Story*. New York: Doubleday, 1977.

Encyclopedia of World Biography. N.p., n.d. Web. 3 Sept. 2010. <http://www.notablebiographies.com/Fi-Gi/Ford-Henry.html>.

Collier, Peter, and David Horowitz. *The Fords: An American Epic*. San Francisco: Summit, 2001.

"Ford, Henry." *Astro DataBank*. N.p., n.d. Web. 4 Sept. 2010. <http://www.astro.com/astro-databank/Ford,_Henry>.

Ford, Henry. "Ford, Henry Quotes." *Quotations Book*. N.p., n.d. Web. 5 Sept. 2010. <http://quotationsbook.com/author/2560/>.

Ford, Henry. "Henry Ford Quotes." *Brainy Quote*. N.p., n.d. Web. 5 Sept. 2010. <http://www.brainyquote.com/quotes/authors/h/henry_ford_2.html>.

Ford, Henry. "Henry Ford > Quotes." *Good Reads*. N.p., n.d. Web. 4 Sept. 2010.

<http://www.goodreads.com/author/quotes/203714.Henr
y_Ford>.

"The Ford Family." *Henry Ford Estate*. N.p., 2004. Web. 3 Sept. 2010.
<http://www.henryfordestate.org/fordfamily.htm>.

Kent, Zachary. *The Story of Henry Ford and the Automobile*. Chicago: Children's Press, 1990.

McCarthy, Pat. *Henry Ford: Building Cars for Everyone*. Berkeley Hts., NJ: Enslow, 2002.

Middleton, Haydn. *Henry Ford: The People's Carmaker*. New York: Oxford University Press, 1998.

Peter Collier and David Horowitz, *The Fords: An American Epic* (1987); Allan Nevins and Frank Ernest Hill, *Ford*, 3 vols. (1954-1963).

Watts, Steven. *The People's Tycoon*. first ed. New York: Alfred A. Knopf, 2005. N. pag. Print.

Weitzman, David L. *Model T: How Henry Ford Built a Legend*. New York: Crown, 2002.

"Bill Gates: Influences in his Road to Success"

Esther Lee
Bergen Academy

Billionaire computer tycoon. Ruthless competitor. Astute predictor of future technology. He represents one of those brief moments in history, such as the gold rush in the mid-1800s, with tens of thousands of Americans rampaging west to find nuggets in streams; the oil age, with wildcatters from Pennsylvania to Texas digging wells to find black gold, when advancements in society, industry, and technology create an entirely changed world. His story is based not on a commodity such as oil or gold, but on technology. Representing the new frontier in creative and technological breakthroughs that affect the masses, the computer and Internet Age's development is in part reliant on this one man who harnessed technology to forever change the world. Among the most important visionaries of the twentieth century is Bill Gates.

Perhaps the most important influence which introduced Bill to technology was his education in Lakeside School, an exclusive boys' academy for grades seven through twelve, because without his education at Lakeside School, Bill may have never been introduced to computer technology. In 1968, the creation of the first minicomputer by Digital Equipment Corporation (DEC) compelled the administration of Seattle's Lakeside School to provide an opportunity for their own students to discover the new technology and language of computers. Before the 1960s, a computer was typically a multimillion-dollar machine comprised of refrigerator-size units linked together by special cables underneath a raised floor in an air-conditioned room accessible only to initiates. Although the minicomputers developed by DEC were more convenient in both size and therefore expense than the dominating IBM systems, the price of a computer was still far beyond the means of a school budget, so Lakeside made the decision to join in a time-sharing relationship.[1] With time-sharing, the user would be able to insert commands and receive answers promptly, rather than typing up a program on a deck of 80-column punch cards, submitting them to an operator, and returning later either with a sheaf of fan-fold computer paper with the results, but more often than not, receiving a single page with a message announcing a mistake in programming logic or a typographical blunder.[2] The local General Electric charged the users $89 per month and $8 an hour for "computer time" for use of its DEC PDP-10 minicomputer. The students at Lakeside were then able to communicate with the computer at the General Electric Office through phone lines with a machine called a Teletype, (which they found ensconced in a tiny office located in the McAlister Hall of Lakeside) made up of a keyboard, printer, a paper-tape punch and reader, and a modem—two "mouse ear" cups that clutched a telephone handset and transferred messages to and from anyone with a similar machine or a time-sharing computer.

In January 1969, Seattle's Lakeside School, ahead of its time, offered computer courses to Lakeside students where Bill and his best friend Paul truly discovered their passion for programming and displayed their instinctive grasp for computers. Very few teachers knew anything about computers so Bill and Paul taught themselves by painstakingly studying all the manuals on computers they could find and learned rapidly, fascinated by all of the possibilities opened to them via the terminal. To Bill, the computer was a challenge to be mastered and describing his first encounter, Bill recalled, "I wrote my first...program when I was thirteen years old. It was for playing tic-tac-toe. The computer I used was huge and cumbersome and slow and

---

[1] Daniel Ichbiah and Susan L. Knepper, The Making of Microsoft : How Bill Gates and His Team Created the World's Most Successful Software Company (Rocklin, CA: Prima Publishing, 1991), 4-5
[2] Stephen Manes and Paul Andrews, Gates: How Microsoft's Mogul Reinvented an Industry—and Made Himself the Richest Man in America (New York, NY: Simon and Schuster Inc., 1993), 25

absolutely compelling."[3]   This passion drove Bill and other students to constantly spend time with computers, and the Lakeside students although beginning as amateurs knowing little of computers, wrote simple programs (also called software), growing in size and complexity, by analyzing BASIC— Beginner's All-purpose Symbolic Instruction Code—and FORTRAN, a programming language used by scientists.[4] With this newly acquired skill, the Lakeside students were able to write instructions, or programs, which the computer responded with solutions to mathematical questions; in addition to his tic-tac-toe game, Bill also set out to formulate programs for practical uses. Together, Bill and Paul underwent thousands of simulations of the DEC PDP-10 in order to ascertain which strategies operated with the least malfunctions, developing an impressive programming prowess.

　　In his Lakeside education, Bill began to excel in his studies. In ninth grade, Bill's school performance changed dramatically when he started receiving straight As. "I came up with a new form of rebellion," he explained. "I hadn't been getting good grades, but I decided to get all As without taking a book home. I didn't go to math class, because I knew enough and had read ahead, and I placed within the top ten people in the nation on an aptitude exam. That established my independence and taught me I didn't need to rebel anymore."[5] Bill became a straight A student as a result of his education at Lakeside School.

　　Due to his experiences at Lakeside, Bill was introduced to the business element of software. When his parents, members of the Lakeside Mother's Club that donated proceeds from an annual rummage sale that solicited directly from the affluent

---

[3] Brad Lockwood, <u>Bill Gates: Profile of a Digital Entrepreneur</u> (New York, NY: The Rosen Publishing Group, Inc., 2008), 16

[4] Jeanne M. Lesinski, <u>Bill Gates</u> (Minneapolis, MN: Lerner Publishing Group, Inc., 2007), 19

[5] Walter Isaacson, "In Search of the Real Bill Gates" *Time*, January 13, 1997.   Retrieved   August   20,   2010 (http://www.time.com/time/magazine/article/0,9171,1120657-4,00.html)

Lakeside parents[6], insisted he pay for his own computer fees upon reaching their limits, Bill explained, "This is what drove me to the commercial side of the software business." He first encountered the "business side" when the "Lakeside Programming Group", consisting of Bill, Paul, and two other Lakeside students, found an unexpected source of virtually unlimited computer use with the newly founded company Computer Center Corporation, a private outfit consisting of a group of computer folk from the University of Washington Computer Center.[7] Monique Rona, a C-Cubed founder and corporate secretary whose son Tom was a year ahead of Bill at Lakeside, made the connection with the school. The C-Cubed computer was undergoing what was known as an "acceptance test," during which the company could make certain the brand-new DEC hardware and software (Seattle's first state-of-the-art Digital Equipment Corporation PDP-10 time-sharing computer, one of the first commercial public-access PDP-10 systems in existence) performed according to specifications. Because during this period, the DEC's PDP-10 software was thoroughly infested with bugs, Computer Center Corporation promised to purchase the machine and possibly deliver to clients such as the Boeing Company—which during the passenger-airline boom of the 1960s had garnered a slew of multimillion-dollar jet contracts and hastily expanded its work force to more than 100,000—once it became reliable. In the meantime, it provided frequent bug reports, deferring payments and the DEC collections department at bay. To submit such reports, Rona wrote the school suggesting that the Lakeside boys help test the PDP-10 computer.[8] Using his business savvy and strong persuasive powers, Bill convinced CCC of their skill and value in DEC programming, and in exchange for computer time, the students were to regularly supply CCC with lists of bugs in the PDP-10 software, including details on the circumstances that caused the computer to crash.

---

[6] Janet Lowe, <u>Bill Gates Speaks: Insight from the World's Greatest Entrepreneur</u> (New York, NY: John Wiley and Sons, Inc., 1998), 7
[7] Daniel Ichbiah and Susan L. Knepper, *6*
[8] Stephen Manes and Paul Andrews, 29

During this time, the students substantially deepened their knowledge of the subtleties of the minicomputer's hardware and software; they filled dozens of pages in the CCC logbook documenting flaws by subjecting the PDP-10 to the most rigorous tests. However, when Bill's programming group breached password protected programs and ventured into unauthorized domains, they were severely chastened by CCC engineers who revoked their computing privileges for the summer. [9] Upon their return, their new strategy was to concentrate on furthering the company: Paul modified the BASIC complier, the program that took the code written by users and converted it into the machine language the hardware recognized; Bill toiled with SYSTAT, a utility program that recorded occurrences in the system; Ric Weiland, a fellow Lakeside student, programmed for a suburban outfit called Logic Simulation, one of C-Cubed's few regular customers. However, the C-Cubed officials began to realize that their initial expectation of selling vast quantities of computer time was simply not going to happen as Seattle entered the throes of a near depression. [10] With few customers and mounting debts, C-Cubed desperately skirted payment on the machines, pouncing on mistakes in invoices, bugs in the software, essentially anything to suspend its lease payments and buy time. In February 1970, when it defaulted on notes of over $60,000, C-Cubed had its assets and receivables assigned to ACQ Computer Corporation of Chicago. The new management kept the computers running twenty-four hours a day, but the inevitable shutdown was finally signaled by a repossession. Gates recalls, "We're sitting there typing at the Teletypes and these guys are coming in taking the furniture and they say to stand up. We're still typing, and the guys are not gonna bring the chairs back..." [11] Although C-Cubed eventually went out of business, not only did it provide Bill and Paul with an apprenticeship in how to use computers, but also an object lesson in how not to run a company. Later,

---

[9] Paul Freiberger and Michael Swaine, Fire in the Valley (Berkeley, CA: Osborne/McGraw-Hill, 1984), 23

[10] James Wallace, Hard Drive: Bill Gates and the Making of the Microsoft Empire (New York, NY: Harper Business, 1993), 33

[11] Stephen Manes and Paul Andrews, 36

Bill and Paul, notorious for their reputations as expert DEC programmers, were contacted by Information Sciences who asked them to write a payroll program for the company COBOL; the two received $10,000 worth of computer hours and made $2,400 in spending money in return. Due to his fateful attendance of Lakeside School, these job opportunities became available to Bill Gates where he learned about the "business side" of computer technology.

Additionally, in the world of technology and personal computers, Bill and Microsoft obviously endured the competition of other companies. However, while the computer industry is based on innovative advances, Bill Gates had an aptitude for eliminating competition, conflicting with his supposed belief. He fiercely made his opinions known in his "Open Letter to Hobbyists" insisting that one had to shield one's own creations, in this case, software programming. One instance of this controversy occurred after Microsoft became an official corporation with employees. Its founders and employees were busy adapting a variant of UNIX (the major operating system at the time) in 1980, but Microsoft had actually acquired the original code in a licensing deal with AT&T and was slowly releasing its adaptation publicly. The product, first dubbed XENIX, would become Microsoft's first and still highly popular word processor, MSWord.[12] Despite his letter, he didn't appear fully opposed to co-opting or relicensing other people's creations and as a result, stealing success that could have been enjoyed by potential competitors of Microsoft.

Microsoft's true emergence as a dominating threat in the computer world occurred when IBM (International Business Machines Corporation), then known by some computer enthusiasts as "Big Blue", was ready to enter the personal computer market. The behemoth of business technology, IBM brought massive investment and credibility to personal computing. Seeking to tap into the growing demand, IBM immediately needed partners for the new initiative. While other companies, Microsoft's competitors included, balked and stalled

---

[12] Alexander L. Taylor III "The Wizard Inside the Machine" *Time*, April 16, 1984. Retrieved August 21, 2010 (http://www.time.com/time/magazine/article/0,9171,954266,00.html)

for more time, Gates saw the opportunity to work with IBM and didn't hesitate. Initially, Gates and Allen wanted to get the contract to deliver BASIC for the new IBM PC, like they had for the Altair, but in an ironic twist, Gates actually sent IBM to a competitor, Digital Research, for the operating system, but when negotiations stalled, (Digital Research delayed reviewing the terms of the non-disclosure agreement) IBM came back to Microsoft. Once again, Gates' decision-making skills that embraced risk proved timely, and again, he promised what he didn't actually have in his possession. Instead, with Allen leading the effort, Microsoft obtained the "Quick and Dirty Operating System" (QDOS) written by Tim Paterson of Seattle Computer Products; however, if Paterson had known that his QDOS was intended for IBM, he may have refused or at least demanded higher compensation. For less than $100,000 (rumored to have been closer to $50,000), Microsoft purchased Paterson's operating system and adapted it, providing IBM with its operating system, renamed PC-DOS, in late 1981 within a matter of months.[13]

As a major partner in IBM, Microsoft now also had an operating system. Gates' and Allen's eagerness for success spurred them to locate and capitalize on their opportunities by adapting someone else's computer code. The purchase and adaptation of Paterson's QDOS had made Microsoft the key software supplier in the personal computer industry and soon after, DOS quickly became the cornerstone for Microsoft's emerging success. Because the IBM PC had been built with "off the shelf" components, meaning that other manufacturers were soon shipping their own "clones" of the IBM PC, Gates and Allen quickly converted PC-DOS, which they had licensed to IBM, to MS-DOS in order to supply the other manufacturers making clones of the IBM PC.

Gates and Allen took advantage of their unique position, based mostly on an operating system developed by someone else, and sensing the profitable potential of using one product to leverage the other, Microsoft relicensed IBM's software to competing clones; this became one of the prized tactics in

---

[13] Brad Lockwood, 40

Microsoft's strategic arsenal as well as his classic lowball pricing that had made Microsoft BASIC a global standard as a language system. [14] Soon the world was overwhelmed with personal computer clones that were manufactured to be like IBM's personal computer, and all of them were running the software that Gates and Allen licensed from Paterson, then adapted for PCs. Whether an IBM, Compaq, or later Dell or Hewlett Packard, if it was an IBM PC clone, it was running a version of the Microsoft operating system, and each manufacturer was paying licensing fees to Microsoft. Tim Paterson of Seattle Computer Products became a huge impact to Microsoft when Microsoft obtained his QDOS operating system and adapted it as their own. Potential competitors such as Paterson influenced Bill and Microsoft greatly, because by employing their ideas and as a result, eliminating them, Bill benefited his own company.

One of the most important companies in the early computer industry was Apple, which created a popular computer called the Macintosh. By incorporating a system called the graphical user interface, or GUI which had originally been developed in the 1960s, even users who knew little about using computers were able to learn quickly. By moving a mouse, a device invented by Doug Engelbart at the Stanford Research Institute in 1963, Macintosh users could point to small pictures, called icons, on the screen to control their computers rather than remembering complicated commands. [15] Apple's innovation influenced Bill to order the creation of the mouse hardware to be used with an upcoming GUI program. Always a risk taker, Bill rested the future of his company on Windows instead of continuing OS/2, a project to develop a more advanced operating system. This new software program called Windows was named for the separate frames users could create on the computer screen, which would feature the graphical user interface (the mouse); with this device, users would operate the computer by pointing and clicking on icons instead of memorizing commands.

---

[14] Randall E. Stross, The Microsoft Way: The Real Story of How the Company Outsmarts Its Competition (Reading, MA: Addison-Wesley Publishing Company, Inc., 1996), 98

[15] Jeanne M. Lesinski, 39

Windows would also allow users to run more than one program at a time—a process called multitasking—and easily move information from one program to another.[16] Apple's Macintosh influenced Bill to realize that developing user-friendly personal computers by using GUI was the next stride in technology. Bill knew Apple may have been the better computer, but he also knew that Apple could not compete with a winning software strategy of licensing to multiple manufacturers creating inexpensive PC clones that ran Microsoft applications. In this instance, Bill again demonstrates his skill in eliminating competition in the ever-growing market by adapting their ideas and innovations and continually increasing his computer empire.

Though Microsoft and Bill have faced challenges over the years, few people would dispute his greatness and his importance to the world's evolution. He has made a tremendous impact on the way we work, communicate, and do business because he is a brilliant entrepreneur who refuses to rest on his laurels; Bill Gates did not succeed in fostering a global revolution in microcomputers by playing it safe and being a people pleaser. The future is what drives Bill Gates and Microsoft—a relentless search for the next bold idea, the next great adventure. Flexibility, experimentation, aggressiveness, risk taking, and an utter disregard for orthodoxy characterize the making of Microsoft; indeed, these same qualities characterize the making of America. When historians look back on the twentieth century, they will undoubtedly rank Bill Gates as one of its most influential people.

---

[16] John Wukovitz, <u>Bill Gates: Software King</u> (London, England: Franklin Watts, 2000), 68

www.ingramcontent.com/pod-product-compliance
Lightning Source LLC
Chambersburg PA
CBHW020353270326
41926CB00007B/416